DANIEL
BOONE

American Pioneer and Frontiersman

Pat McCarthy

Enslow Publishers, Inc.
40 Industrial Road
Box 398
Berkeley Heights, NJ 07922
USA
http://www.enslow.com

Originally published as *Daniel Boone: Frontier Legend* in 2000.

Library of Congress Cataloging-in-Publication Data
McCarthy, Pat.
 Daniel Boone : American pioneer and frontiersman / Pat McCarthy.
     pages cm. — (Legendary American biographies)
 "Originally published as Daniel Boone: Frontier Legend in 2000."
 Includes bibliographical references and index.
 ISBN 978-0-7660-6455-3 (library bound) — ISBN 978-0-7660-6456-0 (pbk.) — ISBN 978-0-7660-6457-7 (epub.) 1. Boone, Daniel, 1734–1820—Juvenile literature. 2. Pioneers—Kentucky—Biography—Juvenile literature. 3. Kentucky—Biography—Juvenile literature. 4. Frontier and pioneer life—Kentucky—Juvenile literature. I. Title.
 F454.B66M37 2015
 976.902092—dc23
 [B]

                                        2014029276

Future editions:
Paperback ISBN: 978-0-7660-6456-0   EPUB ISBN: 978-0-7660-6457-7
Single-User PDF ISBN: 978-0-7660-6458-4   Multi-User PDF ISBN: 978-0-7660-6459-1

Printed in the United States of America
102014 Bang Printing, Brainerd, Minn.
10 9 8 7 6 5 4 3 2 1

To Our Readers: We have done our best to make sure all Internet addresses in this book were active and appropriate when we went to press. However, the author and the publisher have no control over and assume no liability for the material available on those Internet sites or on other Web sites they may link to. Any comments or suggestions can be sent by e-mail to comments@enslow.com or to the address on the back cover.

♻ Enslow Publishers, Inc., is committed to printing our books on recycled paper. The paper in every book contains 10% to 30% post-consumer waste (PCW). The cover board on the outside of each book contains 100% PCW. Our goal is to do our part to help young people and the environment too!

Illustration Credits: ©Shutterstock.com, A-R-T (scrolls); © Thinkstock: Steven Wynn/iStock, p. 4

Cover Illustration: ©Clipart.com
Cover Caption: George Caleb Bingham's painting entitled *Daniel Boone Escorting Settlers through the Cumberland Gap (1851–52)* is a famous depiction of Daniel Boone. He is shown leading settlers through the Cumberland Gap into what would one day be Kentucky.

CONTENTS

Daniel Boone

Chapter 1

DANIEL BOONE TO THE RESCUE

J uly 14, 1776, was a warm, lazy summer day. The people in Boonesborough, a little settlement on the Kentucky River, were relaxing. The Sabbath scripture reading was over, and Daniel Boone was napping. All was peaceful and quiet.

Suddenly, screams shattered the afternoon silence. Then came the sound of running feet and a boy shouting, "The savages have the girls!"[1] Boone sprang from his bed, not even stopping to put on his moccasins. Rifle in hand, he ran to the river's edge, where his thirteen-year-old daughter, Jemima, had been canoeing with two friends.

Joining Boone, Colonel Richard Callaway, father of Jemima's friends Fanny and Betsey, loaded his gun as he ran. Samuel Henderson, Betsey Callaway's fiancé, raced to the river with half his face shaven and the other half covered with soap.

All they saw was the empty canoe on the opposite shore. Apparently, the girls had been kidnapped. Indian attacks were common in the area at that time, so everyone was concerned.

Twelve-year-old John Gass dove into the swift current and swam across the river to retrieve the canoe. The men stood with rifles ready, in case Indians were hiding in the brush on the shore. Tipping the canoe upright, John got in and paddled back across. Boone and four other men jumped into the boat and recrossed the river, to look for clues.

In the meantime, Callaway and several others had leaped onto their horses and galloped a mile downstream to the ford in the river, a shallow place where people could cross. They hoped to cut the kidnappers off there. Boone took charge and divided the group, sending three men upstream and three downstream, in order to pick up the trail more quickly.

The Search Is On

When his group met the riders at the ford, Boone told them to ride as fast as they could to the crossing of the Licking River. Boone was convinced that the Indians were taking their captives north to their towns in the Ohio country.

The other group found the trail, and Boone and his men joined them. They had gone only five miles when it started to get dark. A dog barked suddenly, and the men crept forward silently, hoping they had reached the Indians' camp.

Instead, they discovered nine white men building a cabin. One of the men, William Bush, was a friend of Boone's. The search party decided to camp there until morning. It was now too dark to follow the trail.

John Gass again proved dependable, riding back to the settlement to get needed supplies. Some of the men were dressed in their Sunday clothes, and Boone was still barefoot. In addition to clothes and moccasins, the boy brought food and extra ammunition. He unloaded the supplies; at daybreak, he returned to the settlement.

The Second Day

At dawn, the men were on their way again, accompanied by Bush and two of his friends. The girls had left a trail for the rescuers to follow. Besides breaking twigs and branches along the way, they had managed to tear off little bits of cloth from their dresses and drop them on the path. Betsey had left deep prints in the mud with the wooden heels of her Sunday shoes.

Boone finally decided they would never catch up with the Indians this way. "They're making tracks faster than we are," he said.[2] He decided to leave the trail and cut through the woods on a course parallel to the one he thought the Indians would take.

During his childhood in Pennsylvania, Boone had made friends with the peaceful Delaware Indians living there and had learned the ways of the woods from them. People said he could even think like an Indian. The men of Boone's search party were a little nervous about leaving the track, but they had to depend on his superior knowledge. Nathan Reid recalled, "Paying no further attention to the trail, [Boone] now took a strait [sic] course through the woods, with increased speed, followed by the men in perfect silence."[3]

The pursuers were reassured later in the day when they crossed the trail again and found signs left by the girls. Boone knew they had to catch the kidnappers before they reached their village, or it would be almost impossible to rescue the girls. But by Monday night, they still had not overtaken the Indians, and they had to make camp again.

The Third Day

At first light, they pushed on, crossing Hinkston Creek late that morning. "Here Boone paused a moment," Reid said, "and remarked that from the course [the Indians] had traveled, he was confident that they had crossed the stream a short distance below."[4] Speeding up the pace, the men jogged for the next forty-five minutes.[5]

It was obvious they were closing in on the Indians and their captives. The water in a stream was still muddy from an earlier crossing. A dead snake lay along the trail. And finally, they came upon a freshly killed buffalo, blood still oozing from its hump. Boone told the men that the Indians would stop at the first water they found to cook the meat.

The Rescue

On that third day, the Indians had killed a buffalo and cut off its hump to take with them. A little farther on, they stopped to cook a meal. By now, they had decided they were safe from pursuers.

One of the Indians was tending the meat, Hanging Maw went to get water, and another brave was gathering firewood. The sentry leaned his gun against a tree and went over to the fire to light his pipe.

Jemima heard a slight sound in the brush, and glancing up at a ridge beyond the fire, she spotted her father "creeping on his breast like a snake."[6] Their eyes met and he silently cautioned her to keep quiet. The next moment, a shot rang out.

Fanny, who was watching the Indian at the fire, later said she "saw blood burst out of his breast before she heard the gun."[7] He fell forward into the fire, jumped up, and stumbled into the brush, holding his chest.

Jemima cried, "That's Daddy!"[8] Daniel Boone and two others made hurried shots. The Indians headed for the woods, one of them hurling a tomahawk at the girls. It whistled past Betsey's head, and she ran toward the rescuers. One of them, thinking she was an Indian, raised his gun to club her on the head. Boone grabbed the man's arm and yelled, "For God's sake, don't kill her now when we've come so far to save her."[9] Realizing his mistake, the man fell to the ground, sobbing.

When they were sure the Indians were gone, the men rushed to hug the girls. They were an awful sight, with their clothes torn, their legs scratched and bleeding, and their eyes swollen from lack of sleep and crying. But no one cared.

"Thank Almighty Providence, boys," Boone said, "for we have the girls safe. Let's all sit down by them now and have a hearty cry."[10]

Return to Boonesborough

After eating the buffalo meat that had been roasting over the fire, the group started home. Jemima said she would always remember her mother's relief upon their return: "She both laughed and cried, as she always did when she was over joyed."[11]

Sam Henderson and Betsey were married on August 5. The next year, Jemima married Flanders Callaway, and Fanny was wed to John Holder. All three young men had participated in the daring rescue led by Daniel Boone. Saving the girls from the Indians was just one example of Daniel Boone's leadership, courage, tracking skills, and ability to understand the ways of the Indians.

Chapter 2

INFANT TO FRONTIERSMAN

Daniel Boone's grandfather, George Boone, had lived near Exeter, England, with his family. He was a member of the Quakers, a religious group that emphasized peace. The Church of England was the official religion in Great Britain at that time, and members of other churches were persecuted and ridiculed. George Boone had heard a lot about the American colony of Pennsylvania, which had been founded by William Penn, another Quaker.

In 1713, Boone sent his three oldest children to see what Pennsylvania was like. His sons George, Jr., and Squire, and his daughter, Sarah, went first to Abington, near Philadelphia, where they knew some other Quakers.

From England to Pennsylvania

After receiving good reports about the New World from his children, George Boone brought his wife, Mary, and their other children to settle in Pennsylvania. They joined the "Gwynedd Meeting" of the Society of Friends, another name for the Quakers.

Squire Boone, who would become Daniel's father, was a short, red-haired man with a fair complexion and blue eyes.[1] In 1720, when he was twenty-five, Squire Boone married twenty-year-old Sarah Morgan. She was a large, strong woman with dark eyes and black hair.[2] Squire was a weaver like his father, and he owned a small blacksmith shop. He and Sarah also worked a tenant farm, which was owned by someone else.

Squire Boone built a one-room log cabin in a place called Oley in the upper Schuylkill River valley, near where the city of Reading is today. The house was built over a spring of fresh water. There, Daniel was born on October 22, 1734, the fourth of eleven children. He was named after Sarah's favorite brother, a traveling preacher named Daniel Morgan.

Daniel's Childhood

As a boy, Daniel was small for his age, with sandy brown hair, fair skin, a wide mouth, and bright blue eyes.[3] He was close to his mother. Daniel was always restless during the monthly Friends Meeting. As long as his mother held him by the hand, he stayed by her side, but as soon as she let go, he slipped away and went outside exploring.

His dislike of being confined was really tested during a smallpox epidemic in the area, when Daniel was six years old. The children were forbidden to leave the house, for fear of their being exposed to the deadly disease. Daniel could not stand being inside, so he and his sister Elizabeth, who was eight, decided they would try to catch smallpox on purpose. As soon as they were over it, they reasoned, they would be free to roam the neighborhood again.

One night, after their parents were asleep, the two crept out and ran to the home of a sick neighbor. They crawled in bed with the child, stayed a few minutes, then ran back home.

Sure enough, they were soon covered with red spots. Sarah Boone could not understand how they had caught the disease, but she was suspicious. She looked Daniel right in the face and said, "Now, Daniel, I want thee to tell thy mother the whole truth." He confessed. Luckily, he and Elizabeth survived smallpox and were soon free to roam again.[4]

Learning From the Delaware

One of Daniel's earliest memories was of squatting among a group of Delaware Indians who had come to trade furs for kettles, cloth, and knives.[5] His father and grandfather were always kind to the Indians. In 1728, George Boone had led the rescue of two Indian girls who were being held by a group of white settlers.

Young Daniel was fascinated by the Delaware Indians and was soon following them, asking questions and learning their ways. Some said that all his life, he found it easier to talk to the Indians than to most white people. He learned to think like the Indians, which would help him in many difficult situations throughout his life. Daniel Boone learned to track animals over even the hardest ground, to build a shelter in the forest, and to cook meat so the juices kept it moist.

Daniel's Spelling

When his uncle John, an educated man, complained about Daniel's poor spelling, Daniel's father supposedly answered, "Let the girls do the spelling and Dan will do the shooting."[6]

Daniel's Education

Daniel's uncle George was a surveyor, measuring and marking the boundaries of people's land. Daniel, who loved the outdoors, liked to follow him. Before long, Daniel could draw a good map and figure out the acreage on it.

Daniel would tell his own children that he never attended a day of school in his life. His brother's wife, Sarah Day Boone, taught him to read and write when he was fourteen, but he never had any formal education.

Daniel was influenced by Quaker beliefs and was a peaceful person. Sometimes, though, his temper got the better of him. Once after a day of fishing, he lay down on a flat rock for a nap, his hat over his face. Two neighbor girls decided to play a trick on him. Removing the hat, they dumped a bucket of fish heads and guts onto his face. Daniel did not think the joke was funny. He jumped up and hit both girls in the face.

They ran home crying and soon returned with their mother, who complained to Daniel's mother. Daniel defended himself by saying, "They are not girls. Girls would not have done such a dirty trick. They are rowdies." Mrs. Boone stood up for her son, saying to the girls' mother, "If Thee has not brought up thy daughters to better behavior, it is high time they were taught good manners."[7]

Daniel never went looking for a fight, but he would fight to defend himself. In one boyhood scuffle, he had a tooth loosened. It wobbled in its socket for the rest of his life.

Daniel was chopping wood when he was so small the ax handle was almost as tall as he was. He walked, ran, and swam, and was very strong for his size.

Happy Summers

When Daniel was ten years old, his father bought some pastureland about four miles from home. For the next five summers, Daniel lived in the tiny cabin there with his mother, tending the cattle. The other children stayed at home with their father. In the morning he drove the cattle out into the pasture, and at dusk he drove them back to the cabin for milking.

In the hours between, Daniel roamed the hills and woods. He used a crude weapon he made from a sapling with a cluster of roots at the end to kill small game. He could hurl it at a rabbit from ten yards away with enough accuracy to kill the animal. When he was twelve, his father gave him his first rifle, and he became the main provider of meat for the family. He shot bears, deer, and wild turkeys.

Daniel could clean, dress, and cook a wild turkey. He would hang it by the neck over an open fire and turn it with a stick so it roasted evenly. An Indian had taught him to place a piece of bark under the turkey to catch the drippings so he could baste the turkey as it cooked.

There were times when Daniel became so absorbed in his wanderings and hunting that he forgot all about the cows he was supposed to tend. One time, when he was about thirteen, he was gone all night. By morning, his mother was becoming concerned, so she got some neighbors to help search for him. They found Daniel several miles away, roasting bear meat over an open fire. He had just killed his first bear.

When asked whether he had become lost, he said no. He was sorry to have worried his mother, but he thought because he had been tracking the bear, he might as well kill it before he returned home.[8]

The Teen Years

As Daniel grew into a teenager, his best friend was Henry Miller, an apprentice in his father's blacksmith shop. Henry taught Daniel to repair rifles and traps. The two friends managed to get into their share of trouble. One of their favorite pranks was to take the wheels off someone's wagon and place them in trees or on rooftops.

One night, the two boys wanted to meet some friends for a party. They knew Daniel's father would not approve, so they sneaked out after the family was asleep. They borrowed Squire Boone's best horse and rode it to the party. On the way back, they found a cow sleeping in the path and decided the horse could jump over it. As they approached at a full gallop, the startled cow stood up, and the horse stumbled and broke its neck. The horrified boys left the horse lying there, put the saddle and bridle back in the barn, and crept into bed.

The next morning, Mr. Boone was amazed to find his horse dead in the lane. He always wondered how it had escaped from the barn and broken its neck. He had no idea that Daniel was involved.

By the time he was fifteen, Daniel was the best shot in Exeter. He and Henry were also good trappers. Twice, they took a load of beaver and otter furs to Philadelphia and traded them for gunpowder, flints, and hunting knives for all the men in the family.

How Hunters Dressed

Daniel, at fifteen, had established himself as a hunter and had adopted the dress of the hunters of the time. This was a mix of Indian and European styles. The hunters wore deerskin moccasins, but they were made with European tools. A long hunting shirt, made of linen or linsey, reached well below the waist and overlapped a foot or more in front. Provisions were kept in the front folds of the shirt. A leather belt held the shirt closed, and the hunter's powder horns, knife, tomahawk, and bullet pouch hung from it. Some hunters wore pants, but many, including Daniel, adopted the Indian breechclout. This length of cloth, about a yard long and nine inches wide, passed between the legs and under a cloth belt, with the ends hanging down in front and back. They also wore leggings that stretched to above the knee.

Beaver hats were popular, although some men west of the Appalachians liked fur caps. Daniel could not stand coonskin caps and never wore one. He let his hair grow long, dressed it with bear grease, and pulled it back into a braid or knot.

Deciding to Move

As the years wore on, Daniel began to hear more talk among the men in the family about moving. This became the main topic of conversation as they gathered around the fire in the evenings.

There were several reasons Squire Boone wanted to move. For one, he was in trouble with the Society of Friends. His oldest daughter, Sarah, had married a "worldling," as people who were not Quakers were called. Squire apologized to the Quakers.

However, a few years later, Squire Boone's oldest son, Israel, also "married out." This time, Squire refused to apologize, saying that his children could marry whomever they pleased. He was suspended from the Society of Friends, but Sarah, his wife, remained in good standing.

The scarcity of land in the area was another reason to move. Squire was afraid there would not be enough land for his children to cultivate. The farmland that was available was losing its richness, because farmers at that time did not know much about fertilizers or rotating crops.

In the spring of 1750, Squire made the decision to move. Henry Miller and several Boone cousins decided to go along. When they left, they were still unsure of their destination. Should they go to Virginia, where Squire's sister, Sarah, lived with her husband, or to the fertile Yadkin Valley in North Carolina that they had heard so much about?

When the group set out on May 1, 1750, with Daniel in the lead, they did not yet know where they would eventually settle.

Chapter 3

ON TO
NEW FRONTIERS

When the Boones left Pennsylvania in 1750, fifteen-year-old Daniel guided them through the wilderness. The traveling group included Squire and Sarah Boone, their eight unmarried children, two married sons and their wives, and a married daughter and her husband, one of Squire's grown nephews, and Henry Miller.

They needed three to four big covered wagons and horses to pull them and all the supplies necessary for such a move. They were lucky to travel fifteen miles a day, with good roads and dry weather.

They traveled a route later known as the Allegheny Trail. It crossed the Schuylkill River and led through the Lebanon Valley to the Susquehanna River, near where Harrisburg now stands. After crossing the Susquehanna, they headed southwest, along the curve of the Appalachian Mountains. This route, known as the Virginia Road, had served as a passageway for Indians from the north and south for years. By 1750, it had become the most traveled migration route for settlers.[1]

Some of Daniel Boone's descendants said the family stayed on Linnville Creek, just north of Harrisonburg, Virginia, for at least a year before deciding where to settle permanently.[2]

Daniel Boone's First Long Hunt

In the fall of 1750, Daniel Boone and Henry Miller set off on their first "long hunt." An Indian tradition, the hunt usually lasted through the fall and early winter. Miller later told his son that he and Boone had hunted in the Shenandoah Mountains, then hunted and trapped at Big Lick, on the Roanoke River. They then went east through the Blue Ridge Mountains and south to the Virginia-North Carolina border.

When their hunt ended, the boys visited family in Virginia, then took their hides and furs to Philadelphia, where they sold them and spent the money. Miller later told his family that he and Boone "went on a general jamboree or frolick . . . until the money was all spent."[3] After that three-week spree, Miller decided to give up the hunting life and settle down to make money and save it.

Daniel Boone was perfectly happy. Miller told his son later, "Boone was very profligate [extravagant]... would spend all of his earnings and never made an effort to accumulate."[4] Throughout his life, Boone had problems managing his money. He often owed money, but he always made an honest effort to pay it back.

Settlement in the Yadkin Valley

Not knowing where they would eventually settle, Sarah Boone had obtained letters of introduction from the Friends. These letters were addressed to Quaker meetings in Virginia, Maryland, and North Carolina and would help them become church members wherever they settled. The Boones probably reached the Yadkin Valley in North Carolina late in the fall of 1752.

Squire Boone had traveled alone to the Yadkin as early as the fall of 1750 and bought land there. The Boone family probably built a cabin in the forks of the Yadkin River in late 1751. This was about eighty miles south of the Virginia border, not far from present-day Winston-Salem, North Carolina. About this time, two more of Squire Boone's children were married, and he had plenty of land for the five young married couples and his nephew.

Daniel Boone Grows Into a Man

During this time, Daniel Boone was growing and maturing into a strong young man, not tall, but powerfully built. One man who knew him later referred to him as "a sort of pony-built man," meaning he was not large, but was strong as a horse.[5] He was about five feet eight inches tall and weighed about 175 pounds. He had a high forehead; a long, slender nose; piercing blue eyes; a wide, thin mouth, and dark hair.

He spent the first few years in North Carolina helping his father, now in his fifties, with the farming. However, Daniel was never really interested in working the land. His nephew, Daniel Bryan Boone, later said, "He took no delight in farming or Stock Raising . . . and was ever unpracticed in the business of farming."[6]

Years later, Daniel Boone said that he prayed for rain every day, so he could leave his work in the fields and go hunting.[7] His hunting was not just for fun. It provided meat for the family and money to buy other things they needed. After his first long hunt in 1750, he seldom missed a fall hunt.

Deer were so plentiful that an average hunter could kill four to five of the animals in a day. According to legend, Boone and a friend once shot thirty deer in one day in the Yadkin Valley.[8] Deerskin was an important and valuable commodity, and the word *buck* became synonymous with dollar.

As profitable as deer hunting was, a beaver skin was worth five times as much as a deer's, so Boone also spent a lot of time trapping. Still, his hunting skills helped him develop other talents. Boone became known as one of the best marksmen and hunters in the county. He always did well in shooting matches.

Saucy Jack's Challenge

Boone's skill at winning competitions made him a little foolhardy and once got him into trouble with a Catawba Indian called Saucy Jack. Boone was too good a shot to suit Saucy Jack, and after an afternoon of drinking, Jack vowed to kill him. Luckily, Daniel Boone was not around, but his father, who was in town on business, heard the threat. Grabbing a hatchet, Squire Boone took off in search of the Indian, shouting, "Well, if it has come to this, I'll kill first."[9] No doubt his Quaker friends and relatives would have been scandalized. Fortunately, Jack, who had been warned by friends, fled. That was the end of the matter.

The incident served as a valuable lesson for Daniel Boone, one that would serve him well in his later dealings with American Indians. He later told biographer John Filson that when he was a captive of the Indians, "I was careful not to exceed many of them in shooting, for no people are more envious than they at this sport."[10]

The French and Indian War Begins

As Daniel Boone neared the age of twenty, more and more problems were arising between the white settlers and the Indians. The French and English were struggling over ownership of the Ohio Territory. Control of the forks of the Ohio, where the Allegheny and Monongahela rivers join to form the Ohio River, was a big issue. At that time, when there were few good roads, most trade and travel took place on the waterways.

The French and Indian War had begun. The Indians, who resented the English for taking over their lands, sided with the French. The French controlled what is now Canada, and the

English the eastern part of the present-day United States. Both nations sought to control the whole continent. By now, though, the American colonists were beginning to consider the land theirs, even though they were still British subjects.

In 1754, Colonel George Washington, then an American officer in the British Army, led an attack on the French Fort Duquesne, where Pittsburgh, Pennsylvania, now stands. He was defeated, and the next summer, the British decided to send General Edward Braddock and two regiments of soldiers to take the fort.

Serving with General Braddock

Daniel Boone signed on to drive a supply wagon during Braddock's attack. The wagoners were at the rear of the four-mile-long column stretching along the road. It was an old Indian path, and in order for cannons and heavy wagons to get through, men with axes had to hack their way through the forest and widen the road as they marched.

During the first week, they were only able to travel thirty miles. It took three weeks to travel the one hundred miles to the banks of the Monongahela.

On July 9, 1755, the troops began fording the river. By noon, Boone and the other wagoners splashed across the water. The British Army was an impressive sight, wearing scarlet coats and accompanied by fife and drum. They marched ahead, followed by blue-coated Virginians, who were part of the colonial militia, and groups of frontiersmen, cannons, and wagons.

The French knew they could not hold the fort against the well-trained British troops. Their only hope was to ambush the British Army before it could reach the fort. Fighting alongside the French were Canadians and Indians. Canadian troops blocked the road, and their Indian allies took to the woods, firing on the British troops from behind rocks and trees. The red coats of the British soldiers made good targets. The Americans took to the woods, but Braddock insisted that the British troops remain in rigid military formation. He had no use for the way the Indians fought from behind trees, and he refused all suggestions that his men should fight as the Indians did.

The battle raged for almost three hours. The British had nearly fourteen hundred men at the start, but more than nine hundred were killed or wounded. Many of the Americans were shot by British troops who mistook them for Indians as they slipped through the woods.

George Washington, who had been ill, went to the front. Two horses were shot from beneath him, and a bullet ripped through his hat, but he was unharmed. General Braddock was not so lucky. He was shot and died soon afterward. He had tried to organize a retreat, but the supply wagons that had accompanied the army blocked the passage of the British troops.

Escape

The terrified survivors headed for the river, and some made it to safety. The wagoners had been told to remain with their wagons, but now that would have been suicide. Boone jumped on one of the horses, cut its harness free, and galloped for the river. The Canadians and Indians followed as far as the wagons, then turned back to plunder the rations and scalp the dead. The French marched the British and colonial captives back to the fort, where they were tortured and burned at the stake.

Conflict With an Indian

On his way home, Daniel Boone headed east through Pennsylvania to visit some of his relatives before returning to the Yadkin Valley. As he started across the bridge spanning the Juniata River gorge, he met a large Indian standing in the center. The Indian was drunk and pulled a knife. "[He was] boasting that he had killed many a Long Knife [American hunter], and would kill some more on his way home," Daniel Boone later told Henry Miller's sons.[11]

Boone was unarmed but was determined that this Indian would not kill any more Americans. He charged, driving his shoulder into the Indian's ribs, and knocked him off the bridge to the rocks forty feet below.

Although Boone eventually became renowned as an Indian fighter, he once said, "The truth was, I never killed but three."[12] This was the first. One of Boone's contemporaries wrote, "He never liked to take life, and always avoided it whenever he could."[13]

Dreams of Kentucky

Boone was greatly influenced by one man he met while serving with General Braddock during the French and Indian War. John Findley, a wagoner like Boone, had visited Kentucky. As they sat around the campfire at night, Findley filled young Boone's head with dreams of visiting this legendary land. For years after that, Boone was restless and never lost his determination to go to Kentucky.[14]

But for now, as he returned to the Yadkin, he had other things on his mind.

Chapter 4

MARRIED LIFE
IN THE
YADKIN VALLEY

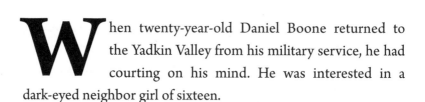

W
hen twenty-year-old Daniel Boone returned to the Yadkin Valley from his military service, he had courting on his mind. He was interested in a dark-eyed neighbor girl of sixteen.

Courting Rebecca Bryan

The first time Daniel Boone and Rebecca Bryan were alone together, he poked holes in her new apron with his hunting knife. They were out cherry picking with some other young people but had found time to be by themselves for a few minutes. Both were shy, and neither had much to say. To hide his discomfort, Boone amused himself by playing mumblety-peg, a game where a pocketknife is thrown into the ground.

Suddenly, the knife pierced Rebecca's new white apron, leaving a long slit. It could have been an accident, but Boone told his children he did it on purpose, to test Rebecca.[1] He wanted to see whether she would get upset or remain calm. When she never mentioned the damaged apron, he decided she was the woman for him.

Rebecca was the daughter of Joseph and Aylee Bryan, who lived nearby in the Yadkin Valley. Boone often hunted with Rebecca's three older brothers, and there were several marriages between their families. The two had first met at one of these weddings.

A legend grew about how Boone met Rebecca. It said that one summer evening he was fire-hunting, using a torch. Deer would freeze, hypnotized by the light, and the glow of their eyes became his target. Supposedly, Rebecca was out looking for stray cows, and her eyes reflected the torch. Boone aimed his rifle at the glowing eyes, then realized this was no deer. Terrified, Rebecca ran off through the woods.

Boone's family did not believe the story. "Without foundation," one of his nephews called it.[2] "As fabulous as it is absurd," wrote his niece.[3]

The family did, however, believe another story that has been handed down about Boone and Rebecca's courtship. Traditionally, a young man would go to the home of the girl he was courting and dress a deer so she could see what a good hunter and provider he was. Boone appeared at the Bryan house with a deer, and outside the house, he cleaned it and cut the meat into chunks, ready to cook. Rebecca then cooked the meat over the fireplace.

The Boones were not as refined as the Bryans, who were well-to-do, so Daniel Boone did not give a thought to the bloody shirt he was wearing when he sat down to eat. Her sisters, and maybe Rebecca herself, laughed and made fun of him.

He ignored them, picking up a cup to drink. Peering inside, he casually remarked, "You, like my hunting shirt, have missed many a good washing."[4]

Boone Gets Married

On August 14, 1756, Daniel Boone and Rebecca Bryan were married in a simple ceremony performed by his father, Squire Boone, who was a justice of the county court. Daniel Boone was twenty-one and Rebecca was seventeen. One of Rebecca's descendants described her as "one of the handsomest persons [I] ever saw."[5] Boone's nephew, Daniel Boone Bryan, said she was "a rather over common sized woman, [with] very mild and pleasant speech and kind behaviour."[6] She had jet-black hair and dark, penetrating eyes.

After the ceremony, Rebecca's sisters served a feast to the guests. Following the tradition of the time, the bride and groom's attendants escorted them to their new home's loft and tucked them into bed. Below, the party went well into the night.

Two months before the wedding, Boone's brother, Israel, had died of tuberculosis. As soon as they married, Daniel and Rebecca Boone took in Israel's two young sons, Jesse and Jonathan, whose mother had died earlier. The boys lived with them until 1773.

The newlyweds lived at first in a cabin on Squire Boone's property. A few months later, they moved to a small farm in the Bryan Settlement, on Dutchman's Creek. Boone built a one-story house measuring eighteen feet by twenty-two feet, with a separate summer kitchen. It was a log house rather than a log cabin. Later he laid a wood floor over the dirt one and put clapboard siding on the outside. They lived there for almost ten years, the longest they were to live anywhere.

Children Are Born

On May 3, 1757, their first child, James, was born. A second son, Israel, joined the family on January 25, 1759. Now the Boones had four children to care for, and Rebecca was not yet twenty years old. Her life was never easy, but she coped with all its demands, such as chopping wood, fetching water, tending crops, and milking cows—her duties as a housewife. She also hunted on occasion when her husband was off on one of his long hunts.

About a year after Israel's birth, Cherokee uprisings in the area caused most people to flee. Boone took his family, his parents, and his younger brothers and sisters to Culpeper County, Virginia, where they would be safe. For a while, he worked as a wagoner, hauling tobacco to Fredericksburg.

The Boones' first daughter, Susannah, was born in Culpeper County on November 2, 1760. After her birth, her father went back to North Carolina alone for his winter hunt. There, he met a slave named Burrell, who worked as a cowherd for a backcountry settler. He told Boone about a rich hunting ground in the Blue Ridge Mountains. The man took Boone and his hunting companion, Nicholas Gist, along an old buffalo trace to a log shelter in a beautiful high meadow. This was where the waters divided, some flowing east to the Atlantic, and the others west to the Ohio.

For years, Boone returned to this cabin on his long hunts. During the 1760s, he became very familiar with this area and went as far west as the valleys of the Holston and Clinch rivers.

Although he sometimes hunted with other Yadkin men, Boone preferred hunting alone. He often spent several weeks in the wilderness, with only his dog and his horse for company. His three-sided shelter was covered with brush, and the open side faced the fire. He carried a Bible, a history book, or his favorite, Gulliver's Travels. He liked to read by the light of the campfire before lying down to sleep on hemlock boughs or dried leaves.

Boone told of a time when he was alone in the mountains of eastern Tennessee. One cold winter night, he was snuggled comfortably under snow-covered blankets, fast asleep. Suddenly, he was awakened as a Cherokee hunter lifted the blanket and exclaimed, "Ah! Wide mouth, have I got you now!"[7]

Boone acted happy to see the Cherokee hunters and welcomed them to his camp. He was not intimidated by them and was at ease with them and their customs. He showed them respect but never betrayed any fear. They soon released him but stole all the furs he had gathered on his hunt.

Boone's relations with the Cherokee were generally good, and he even joined them on an occasional hunt. The story goes that he was once hunting buffalo with a group of Cherokee. They came upon what appeared to be a buffalo trail, but the Indians were skeptical. Catawba Indians sometimes faked buffalo signs to lure the Cherokee into an ambush. "No buffala," one said. "Tawbers [their name for Catawba Indians]!" But a little way down the trail, they came across a large pile of animal droppings. Boone broke down in laughter. "Tawber no make so!" he exclaimed.[8]

A Surprising Homecoming

Boone rejoined Rebecca and the family sometime in 1762, after being gone nearly two years. According to James Norman, who had been with him, Boone found Rebecca cradling a new baby in her arms. He was rather shocked, because he had been away and obviously could not be the father. Upon questioning her, he found out that the baby's father was his brother Ned, who had been taking care of his family during his absence.

The story is substantiated by Stephen Hempstead, a neighbor of the Boones' in their last years.[9] Hempstead claimed that Boone himself told him the story, with Rebecca present. Apparently, Boone forgave her immediately, perhaps out of guilt for leaving her for so long. He accepted baby Jemima as his own, and strangely, became closer to her than to any of his other daughters.

Boone's Carving?

A carving on a tree near the Watauga River was found in the 1770s. It read:

> *D. Boon*
> *CillED A. BAr [killed a bear] on*
> *tree*
> *in the*
> *YEAr*
> *1760*[10]

Historians are still debating whether Daniel Boone carved the inscription, because all examples of his signature show his last name spelled with an e.

Back to the Yadkin

In November 1762, the Boones returned to their home in the Yadkin Valley. Now there were six children, including Israel's two boys. The Yadkin was becoming more densely settled, and game was harder to find. Boone had to go farther and farther from home to hunt. He often went as far as western North Carolina.

By the time James was six, his father was taking him on hunting trips. In the next few years, the little boy showed signs of following in his father's footsteps, becoming an excellent woodsman and hunter. On cold winter nights, Boone would button the small boy inside his roomy buckskin hunting jacket to keep him warm as they lay in front of the campfire.

But Daniel Boone was getting restless. Besides the problem of finding enough game, he was under economic pressure because of debts he had run up for hunting supplies. His father died during this period, which added to his restlessness. His mother went to live with her daughter and son-in-law, Mary and William Bryan, and his three youngest siblings were all married.

Exploring Florida

In the fall of 1765, friends from Culpeper County came to Boone with a proposal. They were heading south to explore the land in Florida that the British had recently gained from Spain. The government was offering free land for those who wanted to settle in the panhandle of Florida. Boone and his brother-inlaw, John Stewart, decided to join them.

They traveled through South Carolina and Georgia to St. Augustine, Florida. There was little opportunity to hunt, and the landscape and climate were discouraging. High water, swampy areas, and hordes of mosquitoes and other bugs made the trip uncomfortable. Stewart became separated from the party and nearly starved before the others found him.

At one point, the whole group became lost in a swamp. They were lucky to be rescued by a party of Seminole, who took them to their camp and fed them venison and honey.

Boone Never Got Lost

When Boone was an old man, someone asked him if he had ever been lost. "No," he said, "I can't say as ever I was lost, but I was bewildered once for three days." The time he and his Florida expedition spent in the swamp before being rescued by Seminole Indians may have been the time to which he was referring.[11]

Home for Christmas

Boone had promised Rebecca that he would be home for Christmas dinner. He timed his homecoming so he walked in exactly at noon, just in time to eat. Rebecca and the children were delighted, until he announced during the meal that they were all moving to Florida. Boone had bought some land in Pensacola.

It seems strange that Boone would want to move to Florida, after the bad experiences he had there, and considering that he made his living mostly from selling animal skins and furs, which would be difficult with the lack of game to hunt in Florida. However, he was restless and ready for a change, and Florida land was available. But Boone had not counted on Rebecca's response. She flatly refused to move. She did not want to be so far from friends and family, and she felt that her husband would not be happy in a land where hunting was not good.

Moving Around

Boone gave in, and in the fall of 1766, he moved the family sixty-five miles up the Yadkin River to Holman's Ford, instead of to Florida. Here, they lived in a cabin on the edge of the Brushy Mountains, where hunting was good.

The next spring, they moved upriver to Beaver Creek in the Yadkin Valley. The year after that, the Boones moved opposite the mouth of Beaver Creek, to the north side of the Yadkin River.

Boone's brother George, who had married one of Rebecca's cousins, moved to the area. So did Ned Boone, who was now the husband of Rebecca's sister Martha. Squire Boone, Jr., and his family, as well as Hannah and John Stewart, soon relocated there. Much of the family was together again.

Two more children were born to Daniel and Rebecca Boone while they lived in these foothills of the Blue Ridge Mountains—Rebecca, born on May 26, 1768, and Daniel Morgan, born on December 23, 1769.

An Exploring Trip

During the winter of 1767–1768, Daniel Boone, his brother Squire, and a friend named William Hill had hunted along the Clinch River in Virginia, then followed the Big Sandy River, hoping to reach Kentucky. They went fifty miles along a buffalo trail to a salt lick. Here, salt was found naturally in the soil, and animals were attracted to it. The youngest of Boone's sons, Nathan, later wrote, "They were ketched [caught] in a snow storm and had to Remain the Winter."[12] They had reached Kentucky, but had not yet found the beautiful country Boone had heard about.

That spring, they returned to the Yadkin, having killed their first buffalo, but Daniel Boone was disappointed. Although they had reached Kentucky, they had not found the paradise his old friend John Findley had told him about.

Renewing an Old Acquaintance

Findley had become a backcountry peddler, selling goods to settlers on the frontier. One day, he showed up on Daniel Boone's doorstep. Findley wanted to go back to Kentucky but needed a guide. Findley said that if they found their way through the mountains, he could guide them to the salt licks and meadows he had seen earlier.

Boone was ready to explore the Kentucky area in search of better hunting grounds, so he did not need much urging. He later told biographer John Filson, "It was on the first of May, in the year 1769, that I resigned my domestic happiness for a time, and left my family . . . to wander through the wilderness of America, in quest of the country of Kentucke."[13]

Chapter 5

CALL OF KENTUCKY

D aniel Boone had dreamed of exploring Kentucky ever since meeting John Findley when he was twenty years old. It was fitting that when he finally realized this dream, it was also because of Findley's influence.

Love of adventure and the fulfillment of a dream were not the only factors in Boone's decision to go to Kentucky. Wildlife was not nearly as abundant in the Yadkin Valley as it had been, and the soil was rocky and thin. There were political reasons, too. The settlers in the area were angry about fees and taxes being levied against them without their consent and about their limited representation in the provincial assembly.

Off to Kentucky

So, on May 1, 1769, Daniel Boone set out with his brother-in-law John Stewart, Findley, and three neighbors. Ten to fifteen packhorses carried their equipment. Boone's nephew, Daniel Boone Bryan, later said, "Boone was the only woodsman, tho' Stewart was pretty good with a gun."[1]

The little group made its way across the Blue Ridge Mountains, then continued north and west through several gaps, or low places between hills, to the Holston River. There, they followed the Warrior's Path straight west, crossing a series of ridges and valleys of the Appalachians. They went to the Clinch River valley and over Powell's Mountain to the Powell River valley. They met twenty men who were clearing land for what would be the westernmost settlement ever tried by white men. Boone's party then followed the river south to the Cumberland Gap, the most famous mountain pass in North America.

Many had passed through the gap before Boone. Probably the first white man to do so was Gabriel Arthur, a young man who was captured in Virginia by Indians from the Ohio country in the late 1600s. When Arthur returned to his home, he traveled through the Cumberland Gap.[2]

After passing through the gap, the trail went north and northwest, through what is now the Daniel Boone National Forest in east-central Kentucky. The trip took more than five weeks. The men built a base camp and called it Station Camp.

Boone Gazes Upon His Paradise

Stewart supervised the building of the camp, while Boone and Findley continued following the Warrior's Path, looking for Blue Lick Town, which had been built by Indians. About twenty miles north of Station Camp and just south of the Ohio River, they found the town abandoned and burned. From the top of Pilot's View, Boone finally gazed on the beauty he had dreamed of for fourteen years. One of his grandchildren wrote that he exclaimed, "We are as rich as Boaz of old [a rich man in the Bible], having the cattle of a thousand hills."[3]

Hunting and Trapping in Kentucky

The men spent the next six months hunting and trapping the abundant game of the area. Buffalo and elk provided meat and leather, which was used to make straps. But deer skins brought the most money back home. When the hunters brought in their game, the camp keepers skinned the deer and scraped the skins, rubbing them until they were soft. They then laid them in stacks across poles and put buffalo or elk skins over them to protect them from inclement weather. They raised them up high so bears, wolves and other animals could not get at them. When they had collected fifty skins, they folded them into a tight bale, called a pack. A horse could carry two packs, worth about a hundred dollars in all.

The men of Boone's party killed what added up to several hundred dollars' worth of deer without being bothered by American Indians. On December 22, 1769, Boone dreamed that he saw his dead father walking toward him. He tried to shake hands, but Squire pushed his hand away with an angry look. The dream made Boone uncomfortable, and he had a feeling that something was going to happen.[4]

Robbed by the Shawnee

As he and Stewart headed back to camp after a day of hunting, they found themselves surrounded by Shawnee from Ohio, whose leader was known as Captain Will. He demanded to see their camps, and the men first took them to some of their smaller caches of hides, hoping the others would hear the commotion and hide the rest of their goods.

They had no such luck, though. When they reached Station Camp, their friends had run away, leaving everything behind. Captain Will's men loaded all the skins on Boone's horses. They made no attempt to capture Daniel Boone and Stewart, but as Boone later related the incident to his children, "In the most friendly manner" they gave each of the white men a little French gun, some shot, doe skin for patch leather, and two pairs of moccasins. This way they could survive the trip back across the mountains.

Captain Will issued a stern warning, however. He said,

> Now brothers, go home and stay there. Don't come here any more, for this is the Indians' hunting ground, and all the animals, skins and furs are ours. And if you are so foolish as to venture here again, you may be sure the wasps and yellow-jackets will sting you severely.[5]

The Indians then rode away with the fruits of eight months of Boone's and Stewart's work.

Boone and Stewart followed them, determined at least to get back their horses. That night, they crept into the Indians' camp and stole back their horses while the Indians slept. They rode through the night until they thought it was safe to stop, then decided to lie down to rest. Immediately, they were surrounded by Shawnee, who laughed at and taunted them.

One cried, "Steal horse, ha?" He put a horse collar with a bell around Boone's neck and made him dance around, while the other Indians whooped and hollered.[6] Then they tied Boone and Stewart together with a leather tug, or strap and forced them to march north. After seven days, they reached the Ohio River, where they planned to release the prisoners the next day.

Freedom

During the night, Boone and Stewart managed to break the leather tug, grab some guns and ammunition, and hide in the canebrake, a dense growth of cane plants, until the Indians left the next morning. It took several days to get back to Station Camp, which was deserted. Farther south, they found their companions, who had decided to go home.

Boone had a pleasant surprise, though. His brother Squire and a friend named Alexander Neeley had arrived with horses and supplies. The Boones, along with Stewart and Neeley, returned to Station Camp. During that winter of 1769–1770, they hunted the buffalo that came to the salt lick, trapped beaver, and explored the land.

A Mysterious Disappearance

Daniel Boone and Stewart hunted together, and Squire Boone hunted with Neeley. Sometimes they would be gone several days. One day in late winter, Boone and Stewart separated to check their beaver traps. Stewart never returned. After several days, Boone found the remains of a campfire and Stewart's initials carved into a tree. There was no other trace of his brother-in-law. It was five years before Stewart's skeleton was found in a hollow tree, along with his powder horn. Boone thought Stewart had been killed by Indians.

Boone was very upset about Stewart's disappearance. He had been a close friend as well as a brother-in-law. When Boone returned to base camp with the news, Neeley decided to go home, and he struck out across the mountains alone.

Daniel and Squire Boone, who assumed Stewart had been captured or killed, remained by themselves in the Kentucky wilderness, continuing their hunt. Boone later told John Filson, "I often observed to my brother, You see how little nature requires to be satisfied."[7] Throughout his life, Daniel Boone was happy living in the woods, with few of the comforts to which most other people were accustomed.

Alone in the Wilderness

The next spring, the brothers were running out of ammunition, so Squire went back to the settlement to sell the furs they had gathered and to get supplies. Daniel Boone stayed alone in the wilderness for three months, with only his dogs and his rifle, "Tick-Licker."[8] At first, he was lonely and missed his family, but later said he "never enjoyed himself better in his life."[9]

Squire returned in July and informed Boone that he was again a father. A son, Daniel Morgan, had been born in December. The brothers hunted through the summer, and in the fall, Squire made another trip to the settlements.

Home to the Yadkin

Finally, in March 1771, the two men loaded up their horses with several hundred dollars' worth of beaver skins and headed home. They got all the way to Powell's Valley, south of the Cumberland Gap, and made camp. Several Indians appeared at their campfire, asking for food. The Boones greeted them as friends, and they talked and ate together. The Indians wanted to trade their cheap guns for the Boones' Pennsylvania rifles. When the brothers refused, the Indians became angry and stole everything the Boones had, including the horses. Their homecoming in May was not the triumphant return they had planned, but everyone was glad to see them.

To Kentucky Again

By fall of 1772, though, Daniel Boone was back in Kentucky with Samuel Tate, Benjamin Cutbeard, and a rash young man named Hugh McGary. An inscription has been found in a cave that served as their base camp on Hickman Creek. "DB. 1773" is carved in the wall, with McGary's name below it.

That winter, people on the eastern seaboard began to get excited about Kentucky. It was getting crowded in the East, and they were hearing stories of the beautiful and fertile lands of Kentucky. The area was then part of the colony of Virginia, and people thought Virginia might begin granting patents on the land there. A few parties of surveyors went to work surveying the land. On the way home that spring, Boone talked to Captain William Russell at Castle's Wood, Russell's settlement on the

Clinch River. The two decided to lead a group of people into Kentucky to settle.

Moving to Kentucky

Boone went home to his family in late April 1773. On May 23, Rebecca gave birth to their eighth child, Jesse Bryan. When Boone informed them they were moving to Kentucky, Rebecca agreed, but their nephews, Jesse and Jonathan, decided not to go. Boone's family was joined by his niece and her husband, Benjamin Cutbeard, Squire and his family, some single hunters, and several other families.

Relatives gathered at the forks of the Yadkin to say good-bye to their loved ones. Rebecca said farewell to most of her family. Boone's mother, Sarah Morgan Boone, was so sad at the thought of Daniel's leaving that she, along with Mary and William Bryan, walked with them the first half day, then returned home.

The Boone party met Russell and others at Castle's Wood. There were no roads. The journey had to be made on horseback, and all belongings had to be transported by packhorse. Little children rode in large hickory baskets, one on each side of a packsaddle. They drove cattle and hogs along with them. The group of forty to fifty people left on September 25, 1773.

Great Britain, which then governed the American colonies, had issued a proclamation forbidding anyone to settle west of the Appalachian Mountains, but no one took it seriously. This attempt was the first by Americans to start a permanent settlement in Kentucky.

The trip was slow, and supplies were being used faster than expected, so Boone sent sixteen-year-old James, along with the Mendinall brothers, to ask Captain Russell for more supplies. They arrived safely and Russell ordered the supplies. He planned to follow the next day, but he sent two slaves, a hired man, and an

Boone's Farewell to His Mother

A young neighbor later described the parting between Daniel Boone and his mother when he left to settle in Kentucky: "They threw their arms around each other's necks and tears flowed freely from all eyes. Even Daniel, in spite of his brave and manly heart, was seen to lift the lapel of his pouch to dry the tears from his eyes whilst his dear old Mother held him around his neck weeping bitterly." It was the last time he ever saw his mother.[10]

experienced woodsman named Isaac Crabtree back with James and the Mendinalls.

A Sad Ending

That night, as the party slept, fifteen Delaware, two Shawnee, and two Cherokee fired on them. Both Mendinalls died immediately. The hired man and Crabtree were injured but escaped to the woods. One slave, Adam, hid under a pile of wood and witnessed the scene. James Boone and Russell's son, Henry, were both shot in the hip and could not get away. A couple of Indians began slashing the wounded boys with their knives.

James recognized one of the Indians as Big Jim, a Cherokee he and his father had met several times. He pleaded for his life, but the Indian responded by tearing off the boys' fingernails and toenails. Soon the two were begging to be killed. When the other Indians got impatient, Big Jim clubbed the boys over the head and shot arrows through their bodies. The Indians then fled, taking the other slave, Charles, with them.[11]

The day before, a young man with Boone's group got into trouble for stealing, so he decided he might as well steal something valuable and go home. He stole a pack of Boone's deer skins and rode off. He soon came upon the site of the massacre. Horrified, he rode back to the camp with the news.

Squire and a few others went back to determine the damage. Rebecca sent two linen sheets with him, in which to wrap the bodies. When they got to the scene, Russell and his men had just arrived. Squire wrapped the Mendinall brothers in one sheet and James and Henry in the other. He buried them all in one grave.

Turning Back

Everyone agreed it was too dangerous to continue the journey. Most of the party returned to their homes. The Boones, however, had sold their cabin and could not just go home. One of Russell's men, David Gass, offered them a cabin on his farm on the Clinch River in Tennessee. They accepted, and Boone hunted there through the fall and winter to support his family.

In the early spring of 1774, Boone decided to visit the site of James's death, in Powell's Valley. He found that wolves had been digging at the graves, but as he dug down, he saw that the bodies had not been disturbed. He unwrapped them and gazed at the body of his beloved son. Then he rewrapped the bodies in his saddle blankets and buried each separately. He tried to disguise the graves so Indians and animals would not bother them.

Chapter 6

SETTLEMENT AT BOONESBOROUGH

J ames's death temporarily discouraged Daniel Boone from settling in Kentucky. Indian attacks that winter in the Clinch Valley sent some settlers scurrying back to safer areas in the east. Still, Daniel Boone never gave up the belief that he would some day live in Kentucky.

The Indians were not the only ones attacking. In April and May 1774, many Indians were killed along the Ohio River in brutal attacks by Virginians. In many cases, the Indians were doing nothing to bother the settlers.

Boone Goes to Warn Surveyors

On June 24, William Russell received a letter from the royal governor of Virginia, Lord Dunmore. He asked Russell to hire two woodsmen to go to Kentucky and warn Virginia surveyors working there of the increased hostilities between American Indians and settlers.

Russell immediately hired Daniel Boone and Michael Stoner. Stoner had been with Boone the previous fall when he attempted to settle in Kentucky, and Boone trusted him. They left on June 27 and spent part of the time locating and surveying possible settlement sites.

They never did find the surveyors they were supposed to warn. Several surveying parties had been attacked and had immediately returned home. Boone and Stoner were very cautious and were always on the lookout for Indians. When they sat down to eat or to rest, they would sit back to back, so they could watch all directions. "Finding the surveyors were driven in by the Indians," Boone said, "I returned home."[1]

Conflict With the Indians

Boone raised a company of volunteers to join the Virginians in attacking the Shawnee at a place called the Levels of Greenbriar, about one hundred fifty miles north of the Clinch Valley. He started out with a number of men, but received a message to return to the valley. His superiors had decided Boone was needed to lead the local defense against the Indians.

On September 23, a war party of Shawnee and Mingo attacked Fort Blackmore, about twenty miles from where Boone's family was staying at Moore's Fort, some fifty miles east of the Cumberland Gap. The Indians were led by Chief Logan, who had formerly wanted peace. That spring, however, some of his own family had been killed in a needless massacre by whites, and his attitude had changed.

The Indians struck several more times in the area, killing several settlers. Because of the leadership he had shown, the men of the community petitioned Captain Daniel Smith, asking that Boone be promoted to captain. Smith passed the petition on to Colonel William Preston, who immediately promoted Boone. Daniel Boone, who had served in the militia all his adult life, treasured this commission and always kept it with him. "I was ordered to take command of three garrisons," he later told John Filson.[2] On October 10, after a battle in which they lost most of their men, the Delaware and Shawnee signed a treaty, giving up Shawnee hunting rights in Kentucky. In exchange, Lord Dunmore promised that the white colonists would remain south of the Ohio River. This ended the conflict known as Dunmore's War.

Boone Obtains Land From the Cherokee

In 1775, it seemed it might be safe to try again to start a settlement in Kentucky. Near the end of 1774, Richard Henderson from North Carolina had asked Boone to help him obtain Cherokee land in Kentucky. The men shared the dream of seeing Kentucky settled, but for different reasons.

Boone wanted good hunting grounds and land for himself and his family. Henderson wanted to start a colony, with himself as governor. Owning a colony would give him power, as well as a lot of money.

The Proclamation of 1773, aimed at keeping colonists out of Indian territory, had made it illegal to settle in Kentucky. However, the British were too far away to enforce it. Even George Washington, a longtime member of the Virginia legislature, saw the proclamation only a stopgap measure to pacify the Indians.[3]

Late in 1774, Boone traveled throughout eastern Tennessee, talking to the Cherokee and telling them about Henderson's offer to buy land in Kentucky. There would be a meeting in March at the Watauga River, where negotiations would take place.

Henderson had also asked Boone to mark a road through the wilderness as soon as the treaty went into effect. Of course, Henderson had no authority to make a treaty with anyone, but neither did the Cherokee have any legal right to the land they were selling. Kentucky at that time was a part of Virginia, so the legal ownership was with the royal proprietors of the colony of Virginia—Great Britain.

The trailblazers were to be paid about ten British pounds for their month's work In addition, they would get first choice of the best land. About thirty to thirty-five men signed up, including Squire Boone, Benjamin Cutbeard, and Will Hays, who had just married Boone's oldest daughter, Susannah.

Boone met with more than a thousand Cherokee at Sycamore Shoals, on the south side of the Watauga River in Tennessee. Henderson was offering fifty thousand dollars' worth of goods—clothing, cloth, knives, and guns, as well as some liquor. Dragging Canoe, son of noted Cherokee chief Little Carpenter, was very much against the treaty. He said that the Americans would soon be claiming other land the Cherokee considered theirs. However, Little Carpenter convinced the others that they should agree to the treaty.

Oconostota's Prophecy

Several days before the signing of the treaty between white settlers and the Cherokee, Chief Oconostota took Daniel Boone aside. Shaking hands, the chief said, "Brother, we have given you a fine land, but I believe you will have much trouble in settling it."[4] Daniel Boone would often remember these words as he faced the many problems that came with trying to create a settlement in a frontier land.

Blazing the Wilderness Trail

The men hired by Henderson began blazing the trail before the treaty was even signed. A young man named Felix Walker kept a journal and mentioned that they generally agreed that Boone "was to be our pilot and conductor through the wilderness."[5] Boone's daughter Susannah and a slave woman belonging to Richard Callaway would do the cooking and keep camp.

Callaway's jealousy of Boone would cause problems over the years. He was bad-tempered and thought himself better than Boone. He resented serving under him.

The men had to widen the Warrior's Path and level it so wagons could use it. The work was difficult, especially in the unpredictable spring weather, which brought late snows, rain, and mud. They cleared vines and overhanging branches, chopped small trees that were in the path, removed dead trees that blocked their way, and built makeshift bridges across creeks.

They went through the Cumberland Gap, followed two buffalo paths, then cut through miles of brush, cane, and weeds. On March 22, they caught their first glimpse of the rolling plains of Kentucky. As Felix Walker wrote, "A new sky and strange earth seemed to be presented to our view."[6] They pushed on another ten miles and camped near a spring.

Indian Attack

Before daybreak on March 25, Indians fired on the company, killing a man named William Twitty and his slave, and injuring Felix Walker. The men quickly built a rough log shelter and put Walker inside. According to Walker, Boone "attended me as his child, cured my wounds by the use of medicines from the woods, and nursed me with paternal affection until I recovered."[7]

On March 27, several men were out hunting and had set up camp for the night. They were drying their moccasins over the fire and were silhouetted against the flames, making perfect targets for the Indians lurking in the forest. Two of the hunters were killed.

While Walker was recovering, Boone scouted the area ahead. He and several others cut a road to a site he had chosen for their settlement on the Kentucky River. They carried Walker on a stretcher between two horses as they moved to that spot.

Building Boonesborough

Boone had chosen a sloping area about two miles long that bordered the south side of the river. A few cabins had already been built before Henderson and his men arrived, and the trailblazers had called it Fort Boone. Henderson changed the name to Boonesborough.

Henderson and Boone wanted to build a large fort, but even though there were eighty people there, it was difficult to get anyone to help with the construction. The men had been hired to build a road or to help transport supplies. That done, they did not want more work. They instead looked for land to claim, hunting for themselves, or plowing and seeding the land. Boone also tried to organize a militia. The men not only had no interest in that, but even refused to stand guard at night.

Food was a problem, too. Most of the settlers had never seen buffalo before, and they killed them just for fun, leaving the meat to rot. Most game had been driven away.

There were only about two hundred settlers in Kentucky, in addition to those at Boonesborough. Henderson held a convention there to draw up a temporary government. Both Daniel and Squire Boone were elected representatives from Boonesborough, along with Richard Callaway and William Cocke.

End of the Transylvania Company

By September, Henderson's Transylvania Company, which had been organized to start the Kentucky settlement, doubled the price of land. Henderson lost any support for his colony he had had among the settlers. By this time, the American colonies had decided they wanted to rule themselves. The Revolutionary War had not begun, but the colonies had set up a body called the Continental Congress. Henderson asked the Continental

Congress to recognize Transylvania as a colony, but was refused. Instead, Congress made the area a county of Virginia.

Boone Brings His Family to Boonesborough

On September 8, Boone and his family arrived at Boonesborough Seventeen young men came with him as well. Boone built a house, with wooden floors, doors, and glass windows. Not many houses on the frontier had glass windows, because they had to be brought from a long distance. Later that month, Richard Callaway returned with about fifty more settlers, including several families. Squire and his family soon followed.

More Indian Problems

Before Christmas, Indians attacked three people near Boonesborough. Arthur Campbell escaped, but one of the boys with him was killed, and the other boy disappeared. Settlers assumed Indians took him. This incident and others like made people worried. Small groups of Mingo, Shawnee, and Cherokee were terrorizing hunters and people who lived in isolated cabins.

The next summer, on July 14, 1776, Jemima Boone and the Callaway girls were kidnapped. On March 7, 1777, a slave working in a field near the fort at Boonesborough was killed by Indians, and his master was wounded. Hugh McGary's stepson was killed and his body mutilated. There were also attacks on Harrodsburg, a settlement about forty miles west of Boonesborough. It was not until April 24, 1777, that Boonesborough was hit again.

Attack on Boonesborough

That morning, the cows refused to go out to pasture, and Boone sent two men to see what was wrong. A group of Shawnee appeared and fired at them. One settler was hit, and an Indian scalped him. Simon Kenton, who would later become a great scout and frontiersman, was standing at the gate and ran out and shot the Indian. About fifteen other men, including Boone and Michael Stoner, rushed to his aid. Boone cried, "Boys, we have to fight! Sell your lives as dear as possible!"[8]

They charged at the Indians, who stood between them and the gate. Boone was shot in the ankle, and an Indian jumped on him, tomahawk raised, ready to scalp him. Kenton crushed the man's skull with his gun, slung Boone over his shoulder, and ran to the fort, bullets crashing around him. Stoner was hit also but made it back to the fort. Four men were injured, and one killed.

Boone called Kenton to him and said, "Simon, you have behaved like a man today. Indeed, you are a fine fellow."[9] It was several weeks before Boone fully recovered, and for the rest of his life, the ankle that had been wounded in the attack bothered him in damp weather.

Hard Times

Chief Blackfish, who had led the attack on Boonesborough, left the settlement alone the rest of the year, but the settlers had other problems. Clothes were worn out, and there was little food. The women followed the cattle to see what they ate, then cooked those greens with salt pork for their families. Meat was the main source of food, because the men could always hunt. By the end of the year, they were about out of salt needed to preserve meat.

The situation was critical in January 1778, Boone agreed to lead a group of men to the salt springs on the Licking River, about fifty miles northeast of Boonesborough. There, they would boil water to make salt for the settlements. Once again, Daniel Boone would have to put his frontier skills to use in order to help his fellow settlers.

Chapter 7

CAPTURE AND ADOPTION BY THE SHAWNEE

A procession of men, their packhorses loaded with iron kettles, left Boonesborough on January 8, 1778, headed for the Lower Blue Licks to obtain much-needed salt for the settlement.

They set up camp and worked furiously, collecting brine, chopping wood, tending the fires, and scraping salt from the kettles. They produced about ten bushels of salt a day. By February 7, they were nearly finished and had sent more than a hundred bushels of salt back to Boonesborough.

While the others made salt, Daniel Boone, his son-in-law Flanders Callaway, and Thomas Brooks hunted game to feed the men. One cold, snowy February day, Boone was hunting alone. He had killed and butchered a buffalo, and loaded three to four hundred pounds of meat onto his horse.

Capture by the Shawnee

Sensing something was wrong, Boone peered through the falling snow and made out the shapes of several Shawnee warriors. He tried to jump onto his horse and escape, but the leather tugs holding the meat were frozen stiff. There was no room for him on the horse with all the meat, so he took off on foot.

Boone was in excellent physical shape, but at forty-two, he could not run as fast as the young warriors. They caught up with him in half a mile. Seeing that he could not escape, Boone leaned his rifle against a tree, signifying surrender. The Indians took him to Chief Blackfish's camp, three miles away.

Boone was amazed to see 120 warriors decorated with war paint in the middle of the winter. He knew Indians seldom went to war at this time of year. Besides the Indians, he saw two French-Canadian traders and a black man named Pompey, who had been stolen from his master as a child.

Meeting Captain Will Again

Looking around, Boone recognized Captain Will, who had captured and robbed him and Stewart eight years earlier in Kentucky. Boone greeted the Indian with apparent joy. "Howdydo, Captain Will!"[1] The Indian stared, then broke into a smile as he recognized Boone. He laughed and said that, apparently, Boone had not heeded his warning about the yellow jackets' stinging.

Boone acted pleased to be with the Shawnee, and they shook hands and greeted him. Blackfish asked about the men at the salt lick. Boone told him they were his men. Blackfish informed Boone that they were on their way to destroy Boonesborough, in retaliation for the death of Cornstalk, a Shawnee chief.

Cornstalk had done everything in his power to peacefully settle the problems between the white settlers and the Indians. In November, he had gone to the American commander at Point

Pleasant on the Ohio River to discuss peace. He and those with him were thrown into a dungeon and later murdered by a group of frontiersmen.[2]

Boone Comes Up With a Plan

Blackfish said they would kill the men at the salt licks on their way to attack Boonesborough. Boone did some quick thinking and came up with a plan. He would persuade his men to surrender without fighting, if Blackfish would wait until spring to make his attack on Boonesborough. By then, Boone said, he would be able to talk the people at the settlement into surrendering as well. The winter weather, he said, would be too hard on the women and children if they were taken prisoner now.

Winter was not a good time to attack, and the Indians' food was also running low. Blackfish agreed not to harm the men at the salt licks if they would surrender. The Indians could then adopt the white men into the tribe and have thirty new warriors.

Boone and the Shawnee arrived at Blue Licks about noon the next day. Callaway and Brooks were still out hunting, but the other twenty-seven men were there. When they caught sight of the Shawnee, they grabbed their guns, but Boone shouted, "Don't fire! If you do, all will be massacred."[3] They laid down their weapons, and the Shawnee moved in.

Lives in the Balance

Blackfish had assured Boone that the men would not be hurt, but many of the warriors disagreed and clamored to kill them. Blackfish called a council and invited Boone to join. Boone sat next to Pompey, who translated to him in a whisper. For hours, Indian after Indian spoke, either for or against killing the captives.

Finally, Blackfish gave Boone a chance to speak. He told the Shawnee that the capture of Boonesborough would be more easily accomplished in the spring. He said that the Great Spirit would be displeased if they killed the young men, because they would make fine warriors and good hunters to provide for the women and children.[4] Boone must have been convincing. The Shawnee council voted 61–59 to spare the prisoners's lives.

Blackfish planned to take the prisoners back to Chillicothe, an Indian town on the banks of the Little Miami River in Ohio country. That night when they camped, Boone was forced to run the gauntlet, which was an Indian custom. Blackfish had promised not to harm Boone's men, but told Boone the promise did not include him. The Indians, holding sticks and clubs, formed two lines and Boone was forced to run between them. They stripped Boone to his breechclout and leggings, and he waited for the signal to start. He would have to run between the lines of Indians, as they hit him with clubs. He knew if he fell, he would be beaten to death. Many who ran the gauntlet did not survive, and others were left crippled for life.

Boone later told a grandson, "I set out full speed, first running so near one line that they could not do me much damage, and when they give back, crossed over to the other side, and by that means was likely to pass through without much hurt." However, as he neared the end, one of the Indians stepped into his path. "The only way I had to avoid his intention," Boone recalled, "was to run over him by springing at him with my head bent forward, taking him full in the breast, and prostrating him flat on his back, passing over him unhurt."[5] This Boone did, and a cheer went up from both the Americans and the Shawnee, who crowded around him and shook hands.

March to Chillicothe

The next morning, the Shawnee and their prisoners were on their way, loaded down heavily. They walked for ten days, through the cold and snow. During the hundred-mile march, they had little food. The Shawnee killed and ate their dogs, but most of the Americans would not eat the meat. Boone told them to chew the bark of the slippery elm and eat the sap oozing from the white oak trees.

When they arrived at Chillicothe, only a few dozen old people and children were there to greet them. The town was built on a ridge near the river and had a spring, fertile fields for growing corn, pastures for horses and cattle, and good hunting and fishing. A big council house was located in the center of town.

That evening, the warriors held a great war dance. The Americans did not celebrate. They were afraid they might be tortured and burned at the stake the next day.

Adoption by the Shawnee

The Shawnee were more interested in adopting the men into the tribe to replace members of their families who had died in battle. Daniel Boone and at least ten others were adopted, some going to other Indian towns to live. They submitted to the adoption, knowing they would get better treatment and might win the trust of their Shawnee families.

One man, Andrew Johnson, had pretended the whole time to be a fool. The Shawnee believed that those who were kind to people touched with madness would have good luck, so a family adopted him and called him Pequolly, meaning "Little Duck."

Blackfish wanted Daniel Boone to be his adopted son, to replace a son who had been killed in the rescue of Jemima Boone and the other girls. Boone was undressed and led to the river, where the squaws scrubbed him, which they believed would remove his white blood. Then the women pulled out all his hair, except for a three-inch tuft on top of his head. They decorated this scalp lock with ribbon and feathers.

After a ceremony at the council house, Boone was considered a true Shawnee. Daniel Boone was named Sheltowee, which meant "Big Turtle."

The News Reaches Boonesborough

After the Shawnee left Blue Licks with the captives, Flanders Callaway and Thomas Brooks returned and guessed what had happened. The crew that was supposed to relieve them arrived soon, and Simon Kenton followed the Shawnee's trail to the Ohio River. Then they all hurried back to Boonesborough with the bad news that the men had been captured.

To Rebecca, the worst thing was not knowing whether her husband was dead or alive, or whether she would ever see him again. There were also some people, including Richard Callaway, who suggested that Boone was a traitor and had sold out to the British. There was no proof, however, that Boone was not loyal to the American colonies. Callaway's accusations may have contributed to Rebecca's decision to take the children and go back to her family. Jemima, however, who was now married to Flanders Callaway, was determined to be at Boonesborough when her father returned.

Some of the captured saltmakers were also suspicious of Boone's motives. He was so cheerful, they thought maybe he was a traitor. Some of the men were so unpleasant that none of the Shawnee wanted to adopt them, so Blackfish delivered them to the British as prisoners of war for a twenty-pound reward.

Trek to Detroit

Blackfish left for Detroit on March 10, taking Boone, the men who had not been adopted, and forty Shawnee. Governor Henry Hamilton, who was in charge of the British headquarters there, paid the reward for the men. He then offered one hundred pounds for Daniel Boone, but Blackfish refused to part with his new son. Boone showed Hamilton his captain's commission, which he kept in a little leather bag around his neck. Hamilton was impressed.[6]

Hostility was growing between England and the American colonies. The English were able to enlist the help of the Indians against these settlers who kept moving west and taking over the Indians' land.

Waiting to Escape

When Blackfish and his group arrived at Chillicothe in April, they learned that Andrew Johnson, who had pretended to be a fool, had escaped. Johnson had traveled to Harrodsburg and told the settlers there that "Boone was a Tory [British sympathizer], and had surrendered them all up to the British."[7] Daniel Boone's acting had convinced Andrew Johnson, as well as Blackfish.

Boone was treated well by his adoptive family, and he felt a great affection for them. He said his Shawnee parents were always "friendly and sociable and kind."[8]

Still, he needed to escape, so he could prepare Boonesborough for the coming Indian attack. He was closely watched and tried to win his captors's trust. One morning while the Indians slept, Boone crept around and took the bullets out of all their guns.

When he finished, Boone made noise to wake everyone, announcing to Blackfish, "I'm going home." "No you ain't," the chief replied. "If you attempt it, I'll shoot you." Boone told him to go ahead, and started walking. The Shawnee grabbed their guns and tried to fire. Boone laughed and walked back, showing the bullets in his hand. "Here, take your bullets," he said. "Boone ain't going away." After this, they showed more trust in him.[9]

Home to Boonesborough

From what others remembered, or were told, Daniel Boone escaped on horseback, rode until his horse was too exhausted to go farther, then continued on foot. He stopped once to kill a buffalo and cooked enough meat for a meal.

Boone's Account of His Escape

Boone never said much about his escape. "On the sixteenth [of June], before sun-rise, I departed in the most secret manner, and arrived at Boonesborough on the twentieth, after a journey of one hundred and sixty miles; during which I had but one meal," he told biographer John Filson. [10]

He reached Boonesborough at last, exhausted and hungry. When he learned that Rebecca had left, he went into his cabin and sat there alone. The family cat jumped into his lap and curled up, as he sat there, depressed. His spirits brightened when Jemima came running into the cabin.[11] He longed to go to Rebecca, but he knew that his first priority was to get Boonesborough ready for the Shawnee attack.

Chapter 8

Siege at Boonesborough

As Daniel Boone prepared Boonesborough to face an attack by the Shawnee, he realized there was a lot to be done.

Finishing the Fort

The fort had never been finished, and what had been built was in disrepair. Boone had the men replace the rotted sections of the stockade and complete the other two sides. They also strengthened the gate and reinforced the corner bastions.

While the men busied themselves with construction, the women molded bullets and prepared bandages. Others cleared brush around the fort and worked in the cornfields.

Messengers were sent to Harrodsburg and Logan's Station, another nearby settlement, asking for reinforcements. Soon ten to fifteen men arrived to help.

Hancock Escapes from the Shawnee

On July 17, a weak cry for help was heard from across the Kentucky River. Sentries who crossed the river to investigate found William Hancock, one of the men who had been adopted by the Shawnee. The man was naked and bruised, and so exhausted from his trip that he could not walk. He warned them that his Indian father, Captain Will, had told him that if the Boonesborough settlers refused to surrender, Blackfish would starve them out, then kill the men and take the women prisoners.

Hancock's return stirred up more suspicion about Boone's loyalty. "Boone when a prisoner promised to give up the fort to the Indians," Hancock told them angrily, "promised every thing."[1]

Raid of a Shawnee Village

By late August, many people were beginning to doubt Daniel Boone. What he did next may have been done in part to assure them that he was not a traitor. He suggested that they raid a Shawnee village not far across the Ohio River. Richard Callaway and others thought the plan was crazy, but thirty men volunteered to go.

They left on August 30, but the next day, about a third of the men thought better of the idea and went back to Boonesborough. Boone and eighteen others went on. Putting on war paint, they started for the Shawnee town. Simon Kenton, sent ahead as a scout, stumbled on two Shawnee, and a whole war party attacked him. Hearing the shots, the others went to his aid, and Kenton got away. The Indians fled, and the settlers were able to steal several horses.

Kenton went ahead to the village on Paint Creek and came back to tell his fellow settlers that there were no warriors or horses there. This indicated to Boone that the Shawnee must be on their way to Boonesborough, so he and his party turned back, deciding to abandon the raid in order to protect their settlement.

Back to Boonesborough

When they got back to the Ohio, they found that the Shawnee had already crossed the river and were now between them and the fort. Boone's party had to recross the river, make their way through dense forests, then cross the river again in order to go around the Shawnee. They rode into Boonesborough on Sunday evening, September 6, 1777, and reported that the war party was on its way.

The Shawnee Arrive

When the settlers got up early the next morning, there was still no sign of the Shawnee. The women went to the spring and the boys watered the stock as usual. Boone and others patrolled the edges of the settlement, anxious to spot the Shawnee. Boone was the first to see them, and he warned the others.

The Shawnee came out of the forest and rode in single file to the meadow. Men from the Detroit militia followed, to escort the settlers back to Detroit. Governor Hamilton of the British headquarters at Detroit still expected Boone to keep his promise and surrender to the Shawnee.

Pompey yelled for Daniel Boone. He answered. Then Pompey shouted that Chief Blackfish had come to accept the surrender of Boonesborough, and he expected Boone to keep his promise. He said he had letters from Hamilton, promising that they would be given safe passage to Detroit.[2] There, they could live as loyal subjects of the British king.

Reunion With Blackfish

Then Boone heard another voice, saying, "Sheltowee, Sheltowee." Blackfish was calling his adopted son. Boldly, Boone walked out the gate to a spot about sixty yards away, still in range of a rifle shot from the fort.

The meeting was friendly. The two shook hands and sat down on a blanket and some Indian boys fanned them with leafy branches. The people in the fort thought Boone was acting very strangely and were afraid he was about to surrender.

Tears streaming down his face, the chief asked, "My son, what made you run away from me?"

Boone answered, "Because I wanted to see my wife and children."

"Well, if you'd asked me, I'd have let you come," Blackfish responded.[3]

The conversation moved on to official matters—the matter of Boone's promise of surrender. Blackfish also gave Boone the letter from Hamilton.

Daniel Boone informed him that he was not in charge anymore, so he must confer with the officers who had taken his place while he was gone. Blackfish understood this, and after smoking a pipe together, they parted.

The men had a long discussion. Finally, Squire Boone said he "would never give up, but would fight till death."[4] Then they unanimously voted to fight rather than surrender.

Boone and Billy Smith, second-in-command, met again with Blackfish that afternoon, sitting on a panther skin spread on the grass. They told the chief they needed more time to consider, and he agreed.

The Americans began to get ready for the battle that was to come. The women dressed in men's hats and coats and paraded back and forth before the gates to make it look as if there were more men. The prisoners had told the Shawnee that they had many more men at Boonesborough than they really did. The men dug a well within the fort, and the women bravely made many trips to the spring, filling every container they could find with water.

That evening, Boone and several other settler leaders met again with Blackfish. He wanted to negotiate further and draw up a treaty. He wanted the chiefs of all the Shawnee towns to meet with them. Boone insisted that all the chiefs from the fort be there, too. He thought it would be safer if he had several of the leaders with him. The settlers hoped the delay would give reinforcements from Virginia time to get there.

A Short-lived Treaty

On Wednesday, the women from the fort prepared a delicious meal for the Shawnee. Then, nine settlers met with eighteen Shawnee. The treaty they came up with sounded fair to all, but Boone did not trust the Shawnee. All the terms of the treaty are not known, but the settlers would have had to swear allegiance to the British king, and in return, would not be harmed by the Shawnee. Both sides signed the treaty, then Blackfish said, "Brothers! We have made a long and lasting treaty, and now we will shake long hands."[5]

The "long and lasting treaty" lasted less than one minute. Each American shook hands with two Shawnee, who made it clear they were trying to take the settlers prisoner. As they wrestled, gunfire broke out from the fort. A warrior hit Boone with the pipe they had smoked, cutting a large gash in his back.

Amazingly, all nine white men managed to escape and made it to the fort alive. Squire Boone took a bullet in the shoulder, which knocked him down, but he got up again and made it inside the gate. Daniel Boone thought they were saved by the volley of gunfire from the fort, which took down several Shawnee.

The Siege Begins

Daniel Boone removed the bullet from his brother's shoulder. It was embedded in the bone, and he had to make a deep incision. Squire was put to bed for a day or so to recover. Even so, he kept an ax by his bed, in case a Shawnee scaled the wall.

Jemima was also hit by a bullet, but she was more embarrassed than injured. It hit her in the backside, and though it was partly buried in her flesh, it did not penetrate the fabric of her petticoat. When she pulled on the cloth, the bullet popped out.[6]

Things were quiet through Wednesday night, but there was steady fighting through the day on Thursday. That night, the Shawnee set fire to some flax drying by the stockade wall. John Holder slipped out and threw water on the fire, managing to dash back inside amid flying bullets.

The Reaction Inside the Fort

The first few minutes of battle were especially terrifying for the children in the fort. Ten-year-old Moses Boone, Squire's son, later recalled, "The women cried and screamed, expecting the fort would be stormed."[7] Livestock ran wildly around inside the fort, kicking up clouds of dust, which mingled with the gun smoke.

Renewed Efforts by the Shawnee

On Friday morning, the settlers became aware that the Shawnee were digging a tunnel from the riverbank toward the fort. They realized the Shawnee planned to tunnel under the fort and blow it up.

That night, the Shawnee, in groups of two and three, began running toward the fort and hurling blazing torches inside the walls. Most of the torches fell harmlessly in the yard, and those that landed on roofs were put out. Squire invented a sort of squirt gun, using an old rifle barrel, which successfully extinguished small fires.

The siege continued, however, and the tunnel was coming closer and closer. Daniel Boone was hit in the upper shoulder by a bullet as he ran across the yard in the fort. Word got out that he had been hit, and the Shawnee started calling, "We've killed Boone! We've killed Boone!"

"No you haven't," Boone shouted back at them. "I'm here ready for you yellow rascals."[8]

On Thursday night, September 17, the fighting was intense and the sky was lit up like daytime. William Patton, who had been on a long hunt when the siege began, was hiding in the woods. He witnessed many screaming warriors running up to the fort with blazing torches and decided it was all over. He went to Logan's Station and announced to the settlers there that the Shawnee had taken Boonesborough.

A Providential Rainstorm

Fortunately, Patton was wrong. Soon after he left, the skies opened up, and the torrents of rain that began pouring down not only put out the fires, but also collapsed the tunnel that the Shawnee had been digging. The next morning, everything was quiet. Thinking at first that it was a trick, the settlers later found out the Indians had deserted their camp and were on the move again.

Fifty brave men, assisted by the women and children of Boonesborough, had held off an army of four hundred Shawnee Indians for eleven days! And they had been prepared thanks to the cunning mind and unfailing loyalty of Daniel Boone.

Chapter 9

Indian Troubles and Lost Land

The siege at Boonesborough was over, but Daniel Boone still could not go to "his little girl," as he always called his wife, Rebecca. First, he had to defend himself against charges of treason at a court-martial.

The Court-martial

Richard Callaway, Andrew Johnson, and William Hancock testified against Boone, claiming that he had been a traitor. Then Boone spoke in his own behalf. He repeated what he had said all along: He had done all the things of which he was being accused in order to save Boonesborough and its people from being killed or taken prisoner by the Shawnee.

The officers in charge deliberated only a few minutes before they decided to acquit Boone on all charges and promote him to a major in the militia. Boone was pleased, of course, but his feelings had been deeply hurt that anyone would question his loyalty to Boonesborough and to the American colonies. After the humiliation of being court-martialed, he never lived permanently at Boonesborough again.

Boone's Court-Martial

There were four charges brought against Daniel Boone: First, that he had handed the saltmakers over to the Shawnee to save himself; second, that he had consorted with the enemy at Chillicothe and Detroit; third, that he had weakened the Boonesborough fort at a time when an attack was expected, by taking the men for the raid on the Indian village on the Ohio River; and fourth, that he had exposed the leaders of Boonesborough to ambush by bringing them to talk with Blackfish and the other Shawnee.[1]

Back to Rebecca

When the proceedings were over, Boone left with Jemima and Flanders. They went back to the Yadkin Valley, where Rebecca and five of the Boones' children were living. Rebecca's uncle Billy Bryan, husband of Boone's sister Mary, had let the family use his cabin.

Boone moved them into a larger cabin, with room for Susannah, Will, and Jemima, as well as Flanders. Boone spent that winter hunting in the Blue Ridge Mountains.

Back to Kentucky

In September 1779, Boone led a group of one hundred settlers back to Kentucky. Among them was the family of Boone's friend Abraham Lincoln, whose grandson and namesake would later become president of the United States.[2] This was the largest group ever to migrate to Kentucky. Most walked during the trip, but a few women and children rode horses.

Settling Boone's Station

The travelers arrived at Boonesborough in late October. Daniel Boone had no intention of returning to live there, but he was forced to remain until his claim on the land to which he was moving was approved by the land commission. On Christmas Day, his family and several relatives left to start a new settlement about six miles away on Boone's Creek. They called it Boone's Station.

The men built "half-faced camps made of boards and forked sticks" to live in during the winter.[3] There was already a foot of snow on the ground, and that winter came to be known as the Hard Winter. Much of the game died, and the stock froze. They never went hungry, though, because Boone had brought along plenty of corn. By hunting, he also managed to provide his fellow settlers with enough meat.

Daniel and Rebecca Boone soon moved to a cabin on Marble Creek, a few miles southwest of Boone's Station. The Boones had taken in six more children, belonging to Rebecca's uncle James Bryan. In order to accommodate the growing family, Boone built a large double cabin. There, on March 3, 1781, the Boones' last child, Nathan, would be born, twenty-three years after their first.

Acquiring Land

As soon as he returned to Kentucky, Boone worked on acquiring land for himself and other settlers. He knew more about the land in Kentucky than anyone else, which put his services in great demand among land speculators.

Boone scouted out land for Thomas and Nathaniel Hart, who had also worked for Richard Henderson's Transylvania Company, which had started the settlement at Boonesborough. They asked Daniel Boone to go to Virginia and buy them land warrants. Several others, including Will Hays, also gave him money to buy warrants for them.

A Great Loss

Boone left Kentucky in late February 1780 with $20,000 in cash. He stayed overnight in a rural inn in Virginia, and when he went to pay the bill, the money was gone. Boone suspected that the landlord had drugged and robbed him, but there was no way to prove it. Boone never got back the money.[4]

He returned to Kentucky and told the men what had happened. Some insisted that he pay them back, which took several years. Others forgave him the amount. The incident had a great effect on him. Of course, some people started rumors that he had faked the robbery and had stolen the money.

Thomas Hart wrote to his brother,

> I feel for the poor people who perhaps are to loose [lose] even their preemptions [the land on which they had settled], but I must Say I feel more for poor Boone whose Character I am told Suffers by it. Much degenerated must the people of this Age be, when Amongst them are to be found men to Censure and Blast the Character and Reputation of a person So Just and upright and in whose Breast is a Seat of Virtue too pure to admit of a thought So Base and dishonorable.[5]

Fortunately, most people agreed with Hart, and Boone's reputation was not ruined by the incident. That November, Kentucky was divided into three counties. Boone was promoted to the rank of lieutenant colonel in the militia of Fayette County. Soon after that, he was elected to serve in the Virginia Assembly and was also elected county sheriff.

More Trouble With the Indians

Meanwhile, Indians and white settlers continued to launch attacks against each other across the Ohio River. Daniel Boone was nearly captured again at his Marble Creek farm, while working in a tobacco shed. Four Shawnee warriors walked into the shed with loaded guns. They looked up at him, perched on the rafters above. "Now, Boone, we got you," one of them said. "Ah, old friends, glad to see you!" he replied.[6]

He gathered up an armful of dried tobacco, dumped it in their faces, and ran for the cabin. They were blinded by the dust and could not catch him. They left, muttering and cursing.

Daniel Boone had another narrow escape in October 1780, but his brother Ned was not so lucky. Their horses were loaded with game, and they stopped to graze the horses. Ned wanted to eat some walnuts, but his brother was worried. "This is a very likely place for Indians," he said.[7] Ned just laughed and began cracking nuts, while Boone shot a bear and went to clean it. He heard shots and turned around to see several Shawnee gathered around Ned's body.

"We've killed Daniel Boone!" one of them exclaimed.[8] They had chased Daniel Boone into the canebrake, not knowing who he was, then sent their dog in after him. He finally had to shoot the dog. The Indians retreated, still thinking they had killed Daniel Boone. They cut off Ned's head as evidence.

Daniel Boone, meanwhile, covered the twenty miles to Boone's Station on foot before morning, and returned with some relatives to bury Ned's body. A wildcat was gnawing on it.[9] The men followed the horse tracks of the attackers, but were too late to catch up with them.

That June, while in Virginia to serve in the legislature, Boone and a friend were captured by British soldiers. They were taken to British headquarters, but were soon released. Boone spent the summer in Kentucky, but was back in Virginia in the fall for the second session of the assembly.

The American Revolution ended with the surrender of British General Charles Cornwallis to American General George

Washington at Yorktown, Virginia, in 1781. Boone went back to Kentucky in the spring of 1782. Though the fighting was over between the British and the Americans, problems continued between Indians and white settlers on the frontier.

The Battle of Blue Licks

In March 1782, three hundred settlers crossed the Ohio and brutally murdered ninety-six defenseless Delaware Indians who had been converted to Christianity. Most were women and children. The Indians retaliated with numerous raids that summer.

In early August, an army of several hundred Indians led by Simon Girty, an American who had been adopted by the Shawnee, crossed the Ohio. One hundred eighty-two Americans rode out to face the Indian army, forty-five of them from the Fayette County militia under Lieutenant Colonel Daniel Boone.

When they came within a few miles of Lower Blue Licks, Daniel Boone felt uneasy. He observed the Indians "concealing their numbers by treading in each other's tracks."[10] He said he thought the Indians were trying to lure them into an ambush, and they should wait for Colonel Benjamin Logan and his men, who were on their way.

Hugh McGary disagreed. "What did we come here for?" he shouted. Turning to Boone, he yelled, "I never saw any signs of cowardice about you before."[11] According to one of Boone's nephews who was nearby, Boone actually burst into tears and answered, "No man before has ever dared to call me a coward."[12]

McGary leaped on his horse and charged into the river, shouting, "Them that ain't cowards follow me."[13] Feeling they had no choice, everyone followed. As Boone rushed up a hill, an Indian rose from behind a stump and Boone fired. Nathan Boone later said about his father, "He believed he had killed

Indians on other occasions, but he was only positive of having killed this one."[14]

Suddenly, the settlers' army was retreating, and there were Indians all around. The whooping of the Indians mixed with agonized screams and the sounds of gunfire. Dust and smoke made it hard to see. Boone sent his men into the woods, hoping they could get to the river under cover, and cross safely. He grabbed a horse and told his son Israel, who was fighting at his side, to mount it and flee. Israel responded, "Father, I won't leave you." Hoping to find another horse for himself, Boone turned away. He heard a moan and scuffling, and saw Israel on his back in the dust, blood gushing from his mouth. Horrified, Boone saw that his eyes were glazed and knew Israel was dead.[15]

Boone ran to the river, which was clogged with floating bodies, plunged in, and made it safely across. He hurried back to tell Rebecca of Israel's death. Daniel Boone could never speak of the Battle of Blue Licks without weeping openly.

Boone later told biographer John Filson, "My footsteps have often been marked with blood. Two darling sons, and a brother, have I lost by savage hands."[16]

Innkeeper and Surveyor

The next year, in 1783, Boone and Rebecca moved to the village of Limestone on the Ohio River, where he became a merchant and innkeeper. There were about a dozen permanent homes there, along with some warehouses and wharves along the river. Rebecca ran the kitchen of the Boone Tavern, with the help of their three slave girls, Easter, Loos, and Cote.

In December 1782, Boone had been sworn in as a deputy surveyor of Fayette County. He did not have much training, and even Nathan admitted that his "knowledge of surveying was limited."[17] Property lines in the area show Daniel Boone's inadequacy at the job.

Boone himself had filed at least twenty-nine claims to nearly thirty-nine thousand acres of Kentucky land. He gave much of the land to his children and was cheated out of much of the rest by unscrupulous speculators (people who bought land cheap and sold it at a huge profit). In order to pay his taxes, he had to sell a great deal of his land.

Reelected to the Virginia Assembly

In 1787, Boone was again elected to the Virginia Assembly, this time by the voters of Bourbon County, where Limestone was located. Now that the American Revolution had ended with an American victory, Boone would be a member of the legislature of a state, rather than of a colony. Kentucky was still considered part of Virginia. Boone, Rebecca, and their son Nathan spent most of the next two years at Richmond, the state capital, while their daughter Rebecca and her husband, Philip Goe, managed the tavern.

Moving Around

During the next ten years, Boone was restless, and the family moved several times, living at Point Pleasant on the Kanawha River in Virginia, at Brushy Creek in Kentucky, and at the mouth of the Little Sandy River where it emptied into the Ohio.

Daniel Boone was hearing rumors about another promised land, the land in Missouri, which was owned by Spain. Now in his mid-sixties, he began thinking seriously of moving west again.

Chapter 10

MISSOURI: THE LATER YEARS

In the late 1790s, Daniel Boone was becoming more and more disillusioned with Kentucky. He had lost much of his land there, and he owed money to a lot of people. He was hearing exciting stories about free land in Missouri, the Spanish territory west of the Mississippi River. He sent his son Daniel Morgan Boone to explore it.

Daniel Morgan Boone Explores Missouri

Impressed with Missouri, Daniel Morgan Boone staked a claim of his own near the mouth of Femme Osage Creek in St. Charles County. With the help of four slaves, he built a small cabin and planted crops. He met Don Zenon Trudeau, the Spanish lieutenant governor of the territory. Trudeau knew of Daniel Morgan's father's fame and was eager to have Boone settle there, knowing that where Daniel Boone went, others would follow.

Trudeau wrote a letter to Boone, offering him 1,000 arpents (850 acres) of the land of his choice. Each male settler he brought with him would receive 400 arpents, plus 40 arpents for each wife, child, and servant. Leaving his slaves to take care of his farm, in the fall of 1798, Daniel Morgan took the letter to his father. He assured Boone that the soil was fertile and the hunting good.

Boone Loses Much of His Kentucky Land

Two noteworthy events had occurred in 1798. On the plus side, a county in Kentucky had been named for Daniel Boone. However, the sheriffs of Mason and Clark counties had sold more than ten thousand acres of Boone's remaining land to pay back taxes.

As Jemima later told her daughter, her father "became somewhat disheartened," and "he pilled [pulled] up Stakes, hearing of the Game and Indians in Missouri."[1] Whatever the reason, Boone decided to move his family to Missouri, and they began preparations the next spring.

Moving to Missouri

Boone and Nathan chopped down a huge poplar tree and made a dugout canoe measuring fifty or sixty feet long and five feet across. It took them until September to finish the boat. They packed it with all their household goods, supplies, and tools. Nathan and Daniel Morgan would take charge of maneuvering the boat down the Ohio River with their mother, Rebecca, and their sisters Susannah and Jemima aboard. Their father took the overland route, driving cattle, horses, and hogs. He was accompanied by Will Hays, Flanders Callaway, and some slaves. Squire and several grown sons went in another boat, and several of Daniel Morgan's unmarried friends also made the trip.

When they stopped at Limestone to pick up Jemima's and Susannah's families, Nathan decided he could not go on. He had to go back and propose to Olive Vanbibber, the girl he had been courting. She and her parents agreed to the marriage, and they were married on September 26. On October 1, the newlyweds set off for Missouri to meet Nathan's family.

Legend has it that the Boone party stopped at the wharf in Cincinnati. Boone was greeted by a large number of people who asked him why he was moving. He is said to have replied, "Too many people! Too crowded! Too crowded! I want more elbowroom!"[2]

A Warm Welcome

The family arrived in St. Louis, Missouri, the first week of October. Henry Dodge, a young man who was there, wrote that Boone "rode a sad looking horse [with] saddle bags, rifle on his shoulder, leather hunting shirt, and a couple of hunting knives in his belt, accompanied by three or four hunting dogs."[3] Boone may not have looked impressive, but he was greeted with great ceremony by both Trudeau, who had invited him to come, and Don Charles Delassus, who had just replaced Trudeau as lieutenant governor. Drums rolled, flags were unfurled, and the Spanish garrison paraded. It was the only time Boone ever received military honors. He was given the job of parceling out land to all the fifteen heads of household who came with him.

Dividing the Land

Boone chose land lying between Daniel Morgan's claim and the Missouri River. Several of Daniel Morgan's unmarried friends claimed land in the same bottom land, which was known for a time as Bachelor's Bottom.

Daniel and Rebecca Boone built their cabin on Daniel Morgan's property, just over the line from their land. Since Nathan did not arrive with the group, he did not receive land, and his father always regretted that he could not give him land as a wedding gift. However, Nathan was able to trade a horse to a man named Robert Hall for his claim in a nearby valley. Jemima and Flanders found a site nearby, too. Unfortunately, Susannah became ill and died just a few days after they arrived. She was thirty-nine years old and left behind ten children.

Squire's wife had refused to move, but he hoped if he built her a nice house, she would come. He started working on a stone house, but two of his sons came from Kentucky and persuaded him to go back home to his wife, Jane. He finally gave in and built her a stone house there.

Daniel Morgan Boone soon fell in love. On March 2, 1800, he married Sara Griffin Lewis, a Missouri girl. They were married in the Roman Catholic Church, the only religion then recognized in the Spanish-owned territory of Missouri.

Life in Missouri

Several of the nieces and nephews the Boones had raised ended up in Missouri, as well as many of the Bryans, Rebecca's family. Nephew Jonathan Bryan built a water mill and was constantly plagued by Daniel Boone's old dog, Cuff. Cuff made a habit of dropping in and licking up the ground meal as it ran down from the millstone into a pewter basin! He even howled when it did not come out fast enough to suit him. Jonathan soon solved the problem by replacing the basin with a coffeepot that was too small for Cuff to stick his head into.

Boone Appointed Syndic

On July 11, 1800, Boone was appointed syndic of Femme Osage. This was like being judge, jury, sheriff, and commandant. He held court under a large tree near his cabin, which became known as the Justice Tree.

He also did a lot of hunting and trapping during these years in Missouri, sometimes with Daniel Morgan and Nathan. Often, though, Boone hunted with one of Daniel Morgan's slaves, a young man named Derry Coburn. Coburn became his regular companion and probably his closest friend. They had a lot in common. Both loved the woods, and they were both quiet men.

Bad Luck and Poor Health

The winter of 1803 was a bad one for Boone. He got his hand caught in a beaver trap and had to take the trap back to camp for Coburn to pry off. His hand was nearly frozen before he was rid of the trap.

The same winter, their camp was robbed by Indians and they lost two hundred skins. This was Boone's last long hunt for a while. Like most outdoorsmen, he had developed rheumatism (pain in the joints) from being out in the damp woods. The problem finally became disabling to the sixty-nine-year-old Boone. That same spring, he heard of the death of his thirty-six-year-old daughter, Levina, in Kentucky. Her husband, Joseph Scholl, soon brought their eight children to live in Missouri.

A few years after the Boones moved to Missouri, Daniel Boone was asked to bring one hundred American families to settle there. He did, and received ten thousand arpents of land for his work.

In Missouri, Boone became reacquainted with some of the Shawnee Indians he had known during his captivity. They remained friends and visited back and forth over the coming years.

In 1805, the Boones' youngest daughter, Rebecca, who had seven children, died from consumption, a disease of the lungs that is now called tuberculosis. Soon after, it was said that her husband, Philip Goe, drank himself to death. Daniel Morgan Boone went back to Kentucky to get five of the couple's children and brought them to live with him and his wife, Sara. They eventually had twelve children of their own.

Boone Goes on Another Hunt

By the fall of 1805, Boone was feeling down, because his health had not allowed him to hunt for two years.[4] Nathan and Daniel Morgan took him on a hunt about seventy miles away to try to cheer him up. On the way back, when they got to the Missouri River, it was in the process of freezing, and they could not get across by boat.

They were disappointed because they wanted to be home for Christmas, but they made camp on the bank of the river. There was a hard freeze that night, and the river was completely frozen. They decided to take a chance and try to walk across. They carried poles and tested the ice ahead of them with each step.

The younger Boones went first. They had just reached the other side, when they heard a splash. Their father had fallen through the ice and was in shallow water up to his armpits. He finally managed to get himself out, and the sons built a big bonfire, took off his clothes, and dried him by it, then carried him home. Luckily, he suffered no ill effects from his dunking in the frigid water.

Losing Missouri Land

By 1806, Boone had heard from his friend Judge John Coburn that his claim to his land would be disallowed. In order to own the land, the settler was supposed to live on it and improve it. Since Boone had built his cabin on his son's land and had not lived on the land he claimed, his claim was ruled invalid.

During the winter of 1808, Daniel Boone planned a long hunt with Derry Coburn. The family tried their hardest to talk Boone out of it, but he would not listen. His nephew, Daniel

Boone Bryan, told him he was "too old to go any more atrapping, and ought now to be staying with his family." He replied, "My wife is getting old and needs some little coffee and other refreshments, and I have no other way of paying for them but by trapping."[5]

Soon after the trip began, however, Boone became deathly ill. He thought he was dying and gave Derry Coburn specific directions about where and how to bury him. He survived, however, and Coburn managed to get him back home.

When he was better, he petitioned Congress to get back his land. He also dictated the story of his life to his grandson for Judge Coburn to use in his quest to get Boone title to the land.

Visits From Old Friends

In 1809, Boone received a surprise visit from his old friend, Simon Kenton. He was so happy to see Kenton that he burst into tears. Kenton stayed several weeks, reliving old adventures. Michael Stoner and James Bridges also stopped to visit while on a hunt. Boone's rheumatism was not too bad at the time, so he and Flanders Callaway joined them in the hunt. Will Hays, Jr., and Derry Coburn also went along, to help the older men. According to Hays, they made it all the way to Yellowstone in Wyoming. They were gone for six months.[6]

War of 1812

When the War of 1812 began, seventy-eight-year-old Daniel Boone was one of the first to try to enlist. He was furious when he was told he was too old.

The young country was again at war with England. Even after the Revolution, the British had continued to encourage the Indians to fight westward expansion by the American settlers. The Americans were also fighting for freedom at sea, because

British ships had been attacking American ships. At one point during the war, it was rumored that an army of Indians was coming to attack the whites in the area. Flanders Callaway decided to abandon his farm. The slaves packed all of the family's belongings into several boats and went downriver to Daniel Morgan's fort. On the way, the boats capsized and everything was lost, including the manuscript of the autobiography Daniel Boone had dictated to his grandson.

Rebecca's Death

The next year, Rebecca became ill after working at the sugar grove for almost a month. Boone managed to get her to Jemima's, but she died a week later on March 18, 1813. She was buried on a grassy knoll on David Bryan's property, where there was a view of the Missouri River.

Boone became very depressed. It was "the Saddest affliction of his life. He oftimes said it was an inexpressible loss," his granddaughter Susanna Callaway said.[7] Another descendant remembered that "After Grandmother Boone died, he [Boone] never was Contented."[8]

Boone Regains Some of His Land

The next year, Congress recognized Boone's claim to land, but gave him back only the original one thousand arpents he had received when he first moved to Missouri.

Angered by this decision, Boone first said he would not take it, but family members talked him into keeping it. He ended up selling this land to pay off old debts.

Many stories are told of Daniel Boone returning to Kentucky to pay all his debts there. Some said they had seen him there, but nearly all the members of his family said he never returned to Kentucky after his move to Missouri. His nephew, Joseph Bryan, said Boone told him a few weeks before his death that he had kept his promise never to set foot in that state again, because it had treated him badly.[9] If Boone did pay these debts, it is likely that someone else took the money to Kentucky for him.

Boone's Later Years

After Rebecca's death, Boone took turns living with his children, spending time at the homes of Jemima, Daniel Morgan, Nathan, and Jesse, who had finally moved to Missouri. He spent a lot of time making powder horns for his grandchildren and friends. These were containers to carry gunpowder, made from animal horns. He scraped the horn thin with a piece of flint, then carved designs in it. His grandchildren remembered sitting on his lap and listening to the exciting stories of his adventures in North Carolina and Kentucky.

Biographer John Peck described Boone in these later years: "His high bold forehead was slightly bald and his silvered locks were combed smooth; his countenance was ruddy and fair. . . . His voice was soft and melodious. A smile frequently played over his features in conversation." Peck had met and interviewed Boone in 1818.[10]

In these final years, Boone enjoyed lying under a shade tree on deerskin, whistling or singing, while enjoying nature, as he always had.

Boone had a coffin built for himself and stored it at Nathan's house, to the horror of some of the grandchildren. He spent time polishing it and said he had "taken many a nice nap in it."[11]

Boone's Portrait Is Painted

One of the last people to meet Daniel Boone was Chester Harding, a young painter who wanted to do a portrait of the old man. Jemima convinced her father to sit for the portrait, but he was so frail that a friend had to stand behind him and hold his head still. "He was much astonished at seeing the likeness," said Harding. Nathan said that when the family saw it, "They all thought it good, except that it did not exhibit the plump cheer, and hence the broad face he used to exhibit in his robust days."[12]

Daniel Boone's Mottoes

Daniel Boone's grandchildren remembered little mottoes he had taught them, including: "Better mend a fault than find a fault"; "If we can't say good, we should say no harm"; and "A man needs only three things to be happy: a good gun, a good horse, and a good wife."[13]

Last Illness and Death

During the late summer of 1820, Boone spent some time with Jemima's family. He became ill with a fever and wanted to go back to Nathan's. The doctor would not let him, but after a few weeks, he made the trip in a carriage. Boone arrived at Nathan's beautiful stone house on September 21. Nathan's wife, Olive, prepared a special meal, and the family said Boone ate too many sweet potatoes. The next day, he still felt full at noon and seemed feverish, so Olive put him to bed. He did not get better. Jemima and her family arrived to see him on the twenty-fifth.

Boone let his family know that this would be his last illness. He asked for his coffin, and when it was brought to his bedside, he thumped it with his cane to make sure it was sound. He told them he wanted to be buried next to Rebecca and discussed funeral arrangements. Jemima cut his hair, saving some locks of it. His granddaughter Delinda, who was Nathan's daughter, brushed his teeth for him. He was almost eighty-six and was proud that he still had them all. He asked Olive to sing for him.

The next morning, he drank a bowl of warm milk, then asked for the family and the slaves to come say good-bye. He had kind words for all of them and said he was going to a happy place and had lived to a good old age. Nathan and Jemima each held one of his hands, and he talked almost to the end. His last words were "I'm going. My time has come."[14] Daniel Boone died on September 26, 1820, a month before his eighty-sixth birthday.

The legislature was in session in St. Louis at the time of his death. When they received word of it, they adjourned for the day, as a sign of respect for the famous frontiersman.

Boone was buried next to Rebecca, as he had requested, and their bodies remained there for the next twenty-five years. At that time, at the request of the Kentucky legislature, their remains were removed to Frankfort, Kentucky, and in 1860, a monument was built there to honor Daniel Boone.

Some people believe the wrong body was removed from the cemetery in Missouri. An anthropologist who examined a cast of the skull believed it was that of an African American.[15]

Chapter 11

LEGACY OF DANIEL BOONE

As happens with many other well-known people, Daniel Boone's legacy has been misunderstood. Many myths exist about his life.

Some Myths About Daniel Boone

Many people have a mental picture of Daniel Boone in fringed buckskin pants and shirt, wearing a coonskin cap. He is often seen as a fierce, loud, bloodthirsty, pushy person, who delighted in hunting down and killing Indians, barking out orders, and bragging about his exploits. Many think he was the first person through the Cumberland Gap, the first white settler in Kentucky, and a great Indian fighter. People have also said Daniel Boone was an atheist, an adventurer who neglected his family for the excitement of the hunt, and a hermit who could not stand being around other people.

Such a picture could not be more wrong. By looking at what Daniel Boone had to say about himself, as well as what others said about him, we can have a clearer picture of what he was really like and what his contributions were.

Correcting the Myths

First of all, the coonskin cap is a myth. Boone could not stand coonskin caps, and usually wore a tall hat made of beaver skins.[1] He did not wear pants made of deerskin. He wore a breechclout, like those worn by American Indians.

Boone was hailed as a great Indian fighter who enjoyed tracking down Indians and killing them. He himself said, "I never killed but three."[2] Those three were killed while defending himself or relatives. A friend said, "Boone had very little of the war spirit. He never liked to take life and always avoided it when he could."[3] The fact was, Boone liked and respected the Indians and made friends with them whenever he could.

"He was evidently kind and benevolent, without any of the ferocity or fierceness which sometimes characterises the border Indian warriors. This accounts for the kindness with which the Indians treated him when a prisoner," said R.W. Wells, who spent three days with Boone in 1817. He recalled, "There was no boasting, no exaggeration, no high coloring. It was plain, simple, and evidently, truthful."[4]

Nor did Boone have a loud, flamboyant nature. "Boone was a reticent man, but not morose," said W.S. Bryan, a relative of Rebecca's:

> He said but little, but what he did say was said in such a way as to create a feeling of friendship and response in those who heard him. In a crowd he would have been selected from among all the rest for his commanding aspect, and yet he would have spoken last of all; but when he did speak all remained silent until he was done.[5]

Daniel Boone was not an atheist. He never joined a church, but he had a deep belief in God. He often attended Baptist services. Many times he carried a Bible with him on his long hunts, and he spent much time reading the Bible in his later years.

Boone's Views on Religion

A letter Daniel Boone wrote to his sister-in-law Sarah Day Boone in 1816 shows his views on religion. He wrote, "all the Relegan [religion] I have [is] to Love and fear god, bel[i]eve in Jes[u]s Christ, Dow [do] all the good to my N[e]ighbour and my Self that I Can, and Do as Little harm as I Can help, and trust on god[']s marcy [mercy] for the Rest and I bel[i]eve god never made a man of my prisipel [principles] to be Lost."[7]

Although Boone was away, hunting, for long periods, his family did not consider him a poor husband or father. One niece said, "His wanderings were from duty. No man loved society better, nor was more ardently attached to his family."[6]

Daniel Boone is sometimes pictured as antisocial, a bit of a hermit who did not want to be with other people. He was unhappy that people thought this. He once said, "Nothing embitters my old age like the circulation of absurd stories that I retire as civilization advances, that I shun the white men and seek the Indians, and that now even when old, I wish to retire beyond the second Alleghanies [sic]."[8]

What People Said About Daniel Boone

Something can be learned about Daniel Boone by looking at what people said about him. J. P. Hale put it this way:

> It is impossible to overestimate the service of the Boone family to this country. When the country comes to build monuments in honor of the heroic men who spent their lives opening up a wilderness and building up a great nation, Daniel Boone and family will doubtless have fitting recognition.[9]

W.L.N. Brown said, "He was a good and great man, a distinguished pioneer of western civilization, and his name and memory deserves a high place in the veneration and esteem of every citizen of the great west."[10]

Simon Kenton, upon hearing criticism years later of Boone's handling of the siege at Boonesborough, said, "He acted with wisdom in that matter."[11]

Boone was definitely important in settling the area now known as the Midwest. His negotiations with the Cherokee led to their selling land in Kentucky to Richard Henderson. He had already located the best land during his explorations.

He was the leader of the crew that cut the Wilderness Road, and he led a group of people to settle in Kentucky. He was responsible for two large parties of settlers' relocating to Missouri.

Boone's knowledge of the forest and the ways of the Indians, as well as his leadership ability, saved the lives of many people—Jemima and the Callaway girls, the saltmakers, and the people of Boonesborough, to name just a few.

But perhaps more than anything else, Daniel Boone should be remembered as a man who had a dream and never gave up until it was realized.

CHRONOLOGY

1734—Born in Exeter Township, Berks County, Pennsylvania, on October 22.

1750—Family leaves Pennsylvania to move west.

1751—Family settles on the Yadkin River in North Carolina.

1755—Serves in French and Indian War with General Braddock in defeat near Fort Duquesne.

1756—Marries Rebecca Bryan on August 14.

1759—Moves family to Culpeper County, Virginia, because of Indian attacks.

1761—Fights to defend North Carolina against the Cherokee.

1765—Explores Florida.

1766—Moves family to North Carolina.

1769—Goes on his first long hunt in Kentucky.

1773—Leads family and friends to Kentucky but turns back after Indians kill son James.

1775—Cuts Wilderness Road, founds Boonesborough, and moves family there.

1776—Rescues daughter Jemima and the Callaway girls from the Shawnee.

1777—Is wounded in Shawnee attack on Boonesborough.

1778—Is captured by the Shawnee while making salt; Siege of Boonesborough; Court-martial.

1779—Leads large group of settlers to Kentucky; Settles Boone's Station.

1780—Is robbed of money collected to purchase land for others; Brother Ned is killed by Indians.

1781—Is elected to Virginia Assembly.

1782—Fights in the Battle of Blue Licks, where son Israel is killed.

1783—Moves to Limestone, on the Ohio River.

1789—Moves to Point Pleasant, Kentucky.

1792—Moves to present-day West Virginia.

1795—Moves to Brushy Fork, Kentucky.

1798—County in Kentucky is named for him; Most of his land is sold for taxes.

1799—Moves family and friends to Femme Osage in Missouri; Is appointed syndic.

1803—Injures hand in hunting accident; He and Rebecca move to son Nathan's farm.

1812—Volunteers to enlist in military during War of 1812.

1813—Wife, Rebecca, dies.

1814—Is granted land in Missouri.

1820—Dies at Nathan's house on September 26.

1845—His and Rebecca's remains are moved to and reburied in Frankfort, Kentucky.

CHAPTER NOTES

Chapter 1. Daniel Boone to the Rescue

1. Draper Manuscripts, 21C28.
2. John Mack Faragher, *Daniel Boone: The Life and Legend of an American Pioneer* (New York: Henry Holt and Company, 1992), p. 135.
3. Ibid.
4. Ibid.
5. Ibid.
6. Ibid., p. 137.
7. Ibid.
8. Elizabeth A. Moize, "Daniel Boone, First Hero of the Frontier," *National Geographic*, vol. 168, December 1985, p. 834.
9. Laurie Lawlor, *Daniel Boone* (Niles, Ill.: Albert Whitman & Company, 1989), p. 94.
10. Faragher, p. 137.
11. Ibid., p. 138.

Chapter 2. Infant to Frontiersman

1. John Mack Faragher, *Daniel Boone: The Life and Legend of an American Pioneer* (New York: Henry Holt and Company, 1992), p. 10.
2. Ibid.
3. Laurie Lawlor, *Daniel Boone* (Niles, Ill.: Albert Whitman & Co., 1989), p. 15.
4. Lawrence Elliott, *The Long Hunter: A New Life of Daniel Boone* (New York: Reader's Digest Press, 1976), p. 11.
5. Lawlor, p. 26.
6. Faragher, p. 16.
7. Ibid., p. 13.
8. Lawlor, p. 15.

Chapter 3. On to New Frontiers

1. John Mack Faragher, *Daniel Boone: The Life & Legend of an American Pioneer* (New York: Henry Holt and Company, 1992), pp. 27, 28.
2. Ibid., p. 28.
3. John Mason Brown, *Daniel Boone: The Opening of the Wilderness* (New York: Random House, 1952), p. 31.
4. Draper Manuscripts, 20C39.
5. Faragher, p. 30.
6. Draper Manuscripts, 22C5.
7. Faragher, p. 31.
8. Michael Lofaro, *The Life and Adventures of Daniel Boone* (Lexington: The University of Kentucky Press, 1986), p. 10.
9. Brown, p. 31.
10. Faragher, pp. 32, 33.
11. Draper Manuscripts, 7C43.
12. Faragher, p. 39.
13. Laurie Lawlor, *Daniel Boone* (Niles, Ill.: Albert Whitman & Co., 1989), p. 45.
14. Ibid., p. 59.

Chapter 4. Married Life in the Yadkin Valley

1. Michael Lofaro, *The Life and Adventures of Daniel Boone* (Lexington: The University of Kentucky Press, 1986), p. 15.
2. John Mack Faragher, *Daniel Boone: The Life and Legend of an American Pioneer* (New York: Henry Holt and Company, 1992), p. 44.
3. Ibid.
4. Lofaro, p. 15.
5. Faragher, p. 43.
6. Ibid.

7. Draper Manuscripts, 2C101.

8. Faragher, pp. 56, 57.

9. Draper Manuscripts, 16C75–16C77.

10. Faragher, p. 57.

11. Draper Manuscripts, 16C56.

12. Faragher, p. 71.

13. Ibid., p. 67.

Chapter 5. Call of Kentucky

1. John Mack Faragher, *Daniel Boone: The Life and Legend of an American Pioneer* (New York: Henry Holt and Company, 1992), p. 76.

2. Ibid., p. 77.

3. Draper Manuscripts, 14CC51.

4. Faragher, p. 79.

5. Draper Manuscripts, 2B188.

6. John Brown Mason, *Daniel Boone: The Opening of the Wilderness* (New York: Random House, 1952), p. 44.

7. Faragher, p. 84.

8. Katharine E. Wilke, *Daniel Boone: Taming the Wilds* (Champaign, Ill.: Garrard Publishing Co., 1960), p. 35.

9. Faragher, p. 85.

10. Ibid., p. 91.

11. Draper Manuscripts, 30C41.

12. Faragher, p. 97.

Chapter 6. Settlement at Boonesborough

1. John Mack Faragher, *Daniel Boone: The Life and Legend of an American Pioneer* (New York: Henry Holt and Company, 1992), p. 101.

2. Ibid., p. 106.

3. Laurie Lawlor, *Daniel Boone* (Niles, Ill.: Albert Whitman & Co., 1989), p. 49.

4. Faragher, p. 112.

5. Ibid., p. 113.

6. Ibid., p. 114.

7. Ibid., p. 116.

8. Draper Manuscripts, 11CC12.

9. Faragher, p. 149.

Chapter 7. Capture and Adoption by the Shawnee

1. John Mack Faragher, *Daniel Boone: The Life and Legend of an American Pioneer* (New York: Henry Holt and Company, 1992), p. 157.

2. Ibid., p. 156.

3. Draper Manuscripts, 11C62.

4. Faragher, p. 159.

5. Draper Manuscripts, 23C36.

6. Faragher, pp. 168–169.

7. Draper Manuscripts, 22C53.

8. Ibid., 30C53.

9. Faragher, p. 172.

10. James Daugherty, *Daniel Boone* (New York: The Viking Press, 1939), p. 57.

11. Faragher, p. 176.

Chapter 8. Siege at Boonesborough

1. Draper Manuscripts, 11C97-99.

2. John Mason Brown, *Daniel Boone: The Opening of the Wilderness* (New York: Random House, 1952), p. 113.

3. John Mack Faragher, *Daniel Boone: The Life and Legend of an American Pioneer* (New York: Henry Holt and Company, 1992), pp. 183, 184.

4. Draper Manuscripts, 24C73, 24C74.

5. Faragher, p. 190.

6. Ibid., p. 193.

7. Ibid., p. 192.

8. Ibid., p. 197.

Chapter 9. Indian Troubles and Lost Land

1. John Mack Faragher, *Daniel Boone: The Life and Legend of an American Pioneer* (New York: Henry Holt and Company, 1993), p. 200.

2. James Daugherty, *Daniel Boone* (New York: The Viking Press, 1939), p. 68.

3. Draper Manuscripts, 31C2.

4. Faragher, p. 208.

5. Ibid.

6. Draper Manuscripts, 23C43.

7. Faragher, p. 212.

8. Ibid.

9. Ibid.

10. Ibid., p. 217.

11. Ibid., p. 218.

12. Ibid.

13. Ibid.

14. Ibid., p. 219.

15. Ibid., p. 221.

16. Ibid., p. 225.

17. Ibid., p. 238.

Chapter 10. Missouri: The Later Years

1. Draper Manuscripts, 21C24.

2. Michael Lofaro, *The Life and Adventures of Daniel Boone* (Lexington: The University of Kentucky Press, 1986), p. 116.

3. John Mack Faragher, *Daniel Boone: The Life and Legend of an American Pioneer* (New York: Henry Holt and Company, 1992), p. 279.

4. Ibid., p. 292.

5. Ibid., p. 295.

6. Draper Manuscripts, 21C45.

7. Ibid., 21C70.

8. Faragher, p. 307.

9. Ibid., p. 316.

10. Draper Manuscripts, 22S259, 22S230.

11. Faragher, p. 316.

12. Ibid., p. 317.

13. Ibid., p. 316.

14. Ibid., pp. 318–319.

15. Draper Manuscripts, 30C79–30C83.

Chapter 11. Legacy of Daniel Boone

1. John Mack Faragher, *Daniel Boone: The Life and Legend of an American Pioneer* (New York: Henry Holt and Company, 1992), p. 21.

2. Draper Manuscripts, 7C43.

3. Faragher, p. 39.

4. Draper Manuscripts, 28C53.

5. Ibid., 29C14.

6. Ibid., 22C35.

7. Ibid., 27C88.

8. Faragher, p. 302.

9. Draper Manuscripts, 28C29.

10. Ibid., 28C114.

11. Faragher, p. xv.

GLOSSARY

apprentice—A young person contracted to work a certain number of years without pay in order to learn a trade.

arpent—A measure of land. Six hundred arpents was a little over a square mile.

Cherokee—A member of an Indian people originally from the southern Appalachian mountains.

court-martial—A trial in the armed forces of a person accused of breaking military laws.

Cumberland Gap—A pass through the mountains where Virginia, Kentucky, and Tennessee meet.

garrison—A place in which troops are regularly stationed.

long hunt—An American Indian custom of spending the fall and early part of winter hunting in order to collect meat and furs for the year.

Long Knife—A term used by American Indians to identify American hunters.

militia—An army made up of volunteer citizens and called in an emergency.

surveying—Measuring and determining the boundaries of a piece of land.

syndic—An appointed government official in Missouri during Spanish rule.

Warrior's Path—A path used by the American Indians to travel through areas now included in Virginia, Tennessee, Kentucky, and Ohio.

FURTHER READING

Books

Brown, John Mason. *Daniel Boone: The Opening of the Wilderness.* New York: Sterling Point Books, 2007.

Calvert, Patricia. *Daniel Boone: Beyond the Mountains.* Buffalo, New York: Cavendish Square Publishing, 2000.

Cavan, Seamus. *Daniel Boone and the Opening of the Ohio Country.* New York: Chelsea House Publishers, 1991.

Faragher, John Mack. *Daniel Boone: The Life and Legend of an American Pioneer.* New York: Henry Holt and Co., 1992.

Hakim, Joy. A *History of US: Making Thirteen Colonies: 1600–1740.* New York: Oxford University Press, 2007.

Santella, Andrew. *Daniel Boone and the Cumberland Gap.* New York: Scholastic Library Publishing/Cornerstones of Freedom, 2002.

Tunis, Edwin. *Frontier Living: An Illustrated Guide to Pioneer Life in America.* Guilford, Connecticut: Rowman & Littlefield Publishing Group, 2000.

INDEX